op

Almond, Philip C.
Rudolf Otto, an introduction to his
philosophical theology

Rudolf Otto

Studies in Religion

Charles H. Long, *Editor*
The University of North Carolina at Chapel Hill

Editorial Board

William A. Clebsch
Stanford University

Giles B. Gunn
The University of North Carolina at Chapel Hill

Van A. Harvey
Stanford University

Wendy Doniger O'Flaherty
The University of Chicago

Ninian Smart
University of California at Santa Barbara
and the University of Lancaster

Rudolf Otto

An Introduction to His
Philosophical Theology

Philip C. Almond

The University of North Carolina Press

Chapel Hill and London

Library of Congress Cataloging in Publication Data

Almond, Philip C.
    Rudolf Otto, an introduction to his
philosophical theology.

    (Studies in religion)
    "Bibliography of Otto's works in English": p.
    Includes bibliographical references.
    1. Otto, Rudolf, 1869—1937. I. Title. II. Series:
Studies in religion (Chapel Hill, N.C.)
BL43.08A65   1984   200'.1   83-19865

ISBN 0-8078-1589-6

Designed by Naomi P. Slifkin

Versions of chapters 1, 2, & 4 originally appeared as
"Rudolf Otto: Life & Work" in *Journal of Religious
History*, 12, 1983, "Rudolf Otto: The Context of His
Thought" in *Scottish Journal of Theology*, 35, 1983,
and "Rudolf Otto and the Kantian Tradition" in *Neue
Zeitschrift für systematische Theologie und Religions-
philosophie*, 25, 1983, respectively. Material from
these articles is reproduced by permission of the editor
of the *Journal of Religious History*, Professor B. E.
Mansfield, the Scottish Academic Press, and de
Gruyter & Co.

to Shalom

"If one subjects everything to reason our
   religion will lose its mystery and its
   supernatural character. If one offends the
   principles of reason our religion will be
   absurd and ridiculous. . . . These are two
   equally dangerous extremes, to shut
   reason out and to let nothing else in."

—Pascal, *Pensées*

Contents

Preface

Rudolf Otto and his analysis of the numinous experience are familiar items of discussion in the modern study of religion, and contemporary accounts of the nature of religious experience invariably and necessarily contain references to his best-known work, *The Idea of the Holy*. Yet there have been surprisingly few studies in English of the full extent of his thought, the last and only full-scale account having been published in 1947. This dearth of studies has been unfortunate, not merely because students of religion have not had easy access to the whole content of Otto's work, but also because *The Idea of the Holy* can only be fully appreciated in the light which Otto's other work casts upon it. My intention is, therefore, to provide a framework upon which a fuller understanding of Otto's thought can be constructed. To this end I have attempted to present a detailed introduction to his thought, and to set it in the religious and philosophical context out of which it arose.

A practical difficulty arose during the preparation of this volume: the inaccessibility of many of Otto's publications, and especially the various collections of essays not translated into English. The appendix gives an overview of the contents of volumes published by Otto and the various revised versions of many of his essays.

I should like to express my thanks to the Council of Hartley College of Advanced Education, Adelaide, South Australia, for granting the sabbatical leave during which much of the research for this book was completed. I am grateful, too, to the staff and graduate students of the Religious Studies

Department at the University of Lancaster for providing me with much stimulation.

Acknowledgments of a more personal sort are also needed. I am indebted to my colleagues Mr. Gunther Kress and Dr. Barry Reay of Hartley College for having read and commented upon earlier versions of several of these chapters, and to Dr. John Clayton of Lancaster University for a number of fruitful conversations. During my time at Marburg I benefited substantially from the kind assistance of Dr. Martin Kraatz, Director of the Religionskundliche Sammlung, and Dr. U. Bredehorn of the University Library. And I express my thanks to Frau Margarete Ottmer and Dr. Ingeborg Schnack, who gave me of their time to talk about Otto. I thank Mrs. Joan Halstead for typing the manuscript. Finally, I am especially grateful to my wife, Brenda, for her support and encouragement.

Rudolf Otto

1
Rudolf Otto's
Life and Work

Introduction

Toward the end of World War I, two books burst upon the
theological scene in Germany. The year 1917 saw the publication of Rudolf Otto's major work, *Das Heilige*; this was
followed in the next year by Karl Barth's commentary on
Paul's Epistle to the Romans, *Der Römerbrief*. Each, in its
own way, set its face against the prevalent secular and rational outlook of the nineteenth century. And both went
beyond the predominant liberal Protestant theology which
had seemed to promise so much but was found wanting in
the context of postwar Europe, the intellectual foundations
of which had been totally undermined by existential dis-
illusionment.

In 1919 Barth saw Otto as a kindred spirit in a struggle
against the dominant school of Ritschlianism. In a letter to
Eduard Thurneysen he wrote:

> This week I read Otto's *The Idea of the Holy* with
> considerable delight. The subject has a psychological
> orientation but points clearly across the border into
> the beyond with its moments of the "numinous"
> which is not to be rationally conceived since it is the
> "wholly other," the divine, in God. It opens the way
> for a basic surmounting of Ritschlianism. Ultimate in-
> sights at least begin to appear, though the subject does
> not quite get moving because of the retention of a the-

ological spectator attitude which is not compatible
with the high degree of the understanding of the
subject.[1]

Otto was at one with the developing Dialectical Theology
initiated by Barth in his recognition of the objectivity and
reality of the source of revelation, that is, the divine, and in
his grounding of religion in that which, of its essence, cannot be totally grasped rationally. But his position was decisively different from Barth's in at least two important ways.
First, although religion is for Otto grounded in the nonrational, this nonrational essence is nonetheless capable of
rational analysis. As we shall see during the course of this
study, the point of connection between the divine and the
human which makes possible some understanding of the
former is the universal human capacity to experience the
divine. The divine is to be grasped in and as the complex
interplay of the rational and the nonrational. After Otto's
death, John Harvey, the English translator of *Das Heilige*,
reported that "he always held that the doctrine of the school
of Karl Barth with its unmitigated assertion of the *Ganz
Andere*, the 'wholly otherness of God,' was a one-sided ab-
beration."[2] And in his final lecture before his retirement
from the University of Marburg, Otto described himself as a
"pietistic Lutheran": a Lutheran in his recognition of the
objective reality of the ground of revelation, but pietistic in
that this recognition was based on the universal human
capacity to have genuine religious experience.[3]

The second difference arises from this and resides in their
respective judgments on the nature and value of religion in
general. According to the Dialectical Theology of Barth, religions and ideologies are merely human attempts at self-
justification and in no way succeed in grasping the divine.
As such, they all come under the critique of Ludwig Feuerbach as illusory projections of man's self-understanding.
Against them there stands, according to Barth, the Divine
Word as the crisis of all religions, theologies, and ideolo-

gies, and as the criterion by which their man-centered and not God-centered character can be judged.[4] In contrast to Barth's implicit assertion that Christianity is the sole and absolute bearer of religious truth, Otto's primary concern is to establish the validity of religion *in general* in opposition to all attempts to reduce it to a mere function of individual psychology or a product of group psychology—in short, in opposition to all attempts to explain it in solely naturalistic or materialistic terms. For Otto, religion in general is ultimately and only referrable to a preconceptual and pre-ethical nonrational and irreducible ground which cannot be eliminated without the loss of religion's inner essence. Therefore Christianity can only be understood in relation to religion in general and in comparison with other manifestations of the nonrational essence of religion. Christianity needs to be understood, Otto writes, "in its natural affinity and connection with religion in general, i.e., against a background of comparative religion and the history of religion."[5]

The effect of Barth's work was enormous, initiating as it did a new theological epoch. Assuredly, for the major part of Otto's time at the University of Marburg, Dialectical Theology overshadowed all else. Ernst Benz reports that Otto's lectures were ridiculed by students committed to the existentialist theology of Rudolf Bultmann, and that the religious collection founded by Otto was referred to as the "heathen temple" by those students for whom Dialectical Theology entailed the unnecessariness and superfluity of the history and comparison of religions. The polemical situation which resulted was, along with Otto's increasing ill health, an influence on his decision to retire early, in March 1929.[6]

The predominance of Dialectical Theology curtailed Otto's influence on the development of German theology during the first half of the twentieth century. Certainly, during the first few years of his tenure in the chair of Systematic Theology at Marburg, he was highly regarded by both colleagues and students. But when Dialectical Theology became the vogue, from 1921 onward, there developed a rift within the theology faculty. Students flocked to hear Bultmann, and therefore Martin Heidegger also, leaving Otto with fewer and fewer.[7]

As has often been pointed out, there was talk of "Barthians" quite soon after Barth's *Der Römerbrief*, but there were scarcely any "Ottonians." This was, in part, due to Otto's personality. For those who knew him closely he was undoubtedly an impressive person. As Joachim Wach recalls:

> Rudolf Otto was an imposing figure. He held himself very straight. His movements were measured. His sharply cut features remained serious and scarcely altered even when joking. The color of his skin was yellowish-white and testified to past illness. Otto had contracted a tropical illness in India which forced him to always husband his strength strictly. His hair was white and cut short. A small white moustache covered his upper lip. Most fascinating of all were his steel-blue eyes. They had a certain rigidity about them, and it was often as if, when he spoke, he saw something to which others had no access. . . . Something mysterious surrounded him. Familiarity was the last thing a visitor would have expected of him or he himself would have encouraged. The students, who followed his lectures spellbound, called him "der Heilige" (the Saint).[8]

Many were undoubtedly attracted by the power of his personality, but many were likewise deterred. Students found him difficult to approach and disliked his apparently Victorian character.[9] He was retiring and uncommunicative;[10] his ascetic nature was also reinforced by a strictness in morality. Otto was clearly aware of the way in which he remained aloof from people. At the end of his life, although he was certain that his discovery of the numinous experience would be a permanent contribution to the study of religion, he was unhappy that, because of his unapproachability, he had not been completely successful as a teacher.[11] Those few who were able to pierce his outward reserve attest, however, to his warmth and congeniality.

Otto's deep piety cannot be doubted. He was a man of simple yet deep faith without any affectation or inhibition. Yet, as his scholarly work shows, he was also a man who struggled to retain that faith. He was firmly committed to Christianity and yet fully aware of the claims made by other traditions upon the exclusivity of the truth of Christianity. Indeed, throughout his later years he longed for an experience comparable to that of Paul on the road to Damascus to occur as a resolution of his inner struggle.[12]

Setting aside the complexities of Otto's personality and the situation in Marburg, several other reasons may also be suggested for the predominance of Barth and those theological positions intimately related to his. One is the sheer intellectual power and literary vigor with which Barth asserted the exclusive claims of the Christian Gospel. This was in marked contrast to Otto's much less assertive yet (in principle, at least) perhaps ultimately more convincing weighing of Christianity in the balance of religion in general. Although Otto wrote for students of theology, his work was to appeal more to students of *Religionswissenschaft* than to those seeking an absolute ground for their own commitment to Christianity. Furthermore, the predominance of Dialectical Theology must in part be attributed to Barth's progressively forthright denunciation of the validity of a theology grounded in philosophy, or to Bultmann's superimposition of theology on a Heideggerian framework, both of which were more in keeping with the contemporary *Zeitgeist* than was Otto's much criticized dependence on the early twentieth-century revival of the Kantianism of Jakob Fries.

Be that as it may, let me not give the impression that I underestimate the importance of Otto's work. From the beginning *Das Heilige* was recognized as a work of the first importance, one which, according to Adolf Harnack, was comparable with Friedrich Schleiermacher's *Speeches on Religion*: "When Schleiermacher led 'religion' one hundred and thirty years ago, and in our day Otto led 'the Holy' out of ensnaring and enveloping connections, a shower of illumination and liberation went through German evangelical Christians."[13]

The popularity and influence of *Das Heilige* is also attested to by the fact that, apart from the numerous German editions, within twelve years of its initial publication it was translated into seven other languages: English in 1923, Swedish in 1924, Spanish in 1925, Italian in 1926, Japanese in 1927, Dutch in 1928, and French in 1929. The publication of *Das Heilige* consequently established Otto's reputation throughout the scholarly world. Indeed, it has been suggested quite rightly that Otto's book had greater success outside Germany than within it.[14] Certainly the English translation, *The Idea of the Holy*, was exceptionally well received. A. Barrett-Brown in *The Friend* called it "the most significant contribution to the understanding of the nature of religion since William James delivered his Gifford Lectures on *The Varieties of Religious Experience* some twenty years ago."[15] And William Paton in *The Guardian* on May 21, 1925, referred to it as "a great book," "a brilliant book."[16]

The Idea of the Holy became so influential that it overshadowed Otto's other works—to such an extent that most of them have been consigned to oblivion. This is unfortunate because, aside from the intrinsic interest and importance some of them possess, to ignore them is to risk misunderstanding much in *The Idea of the Holy*. To be sure, this work is the fulcrum of Otto's work on religion; his earlier work points to it, and his later work is in substance a development of it. Still, *The Idea of the Holy* can only be fully appreciated from the perspective of Otto's earlier writings. Moreover, as I hope to show, much light can be cast upon it by an examination of those works which arose out of it. I do not intend to imply that Otto's writings form a continuous and coherent whole, although I suspect that Otto himself believed this to be the case. Rather, I suggest that the conjunction of philosophical, phenomenological, and theological concerns evident in the pages of *The Idea of the Holy* all have their origins in Otto's earlier writings. Consideration of these cannot but be illuminating, particularly if it can be demonstrated that the marriage of these various concerns is not always a happy one.

Consistency is not always to be found in Otto's solutions to a number of issues. Nevertheless, what lends his writings an overall appearance of unity is the persistent examination of certain problems which occupied him throughout his academic career and his intellectual development. First, there is the problem of the relationship between religion and the natural and social sciences. Otto continually attacked the pretensions of naturalistic and materialistic explanations of the world, and therefore of religion. This emphasis is revealed in his earliest works on the autonomy of religion, its independence and irreducibility, and its objective nature. Furthermore, for Otto the essence of religion is to be found in its nonrational elements, and these, together with rational elements, constitute (to use his metaphor) its warp and woof. Otto's writings therefore show an abiding concern not only for the nonrational and rational elements in themselves, but also for the nature of their conjunction and the means by which this is effected. Finally, there is the question of the validity of particular religious traditions. Certainly for Otto Christianity remains superior to other religions, though his position on the superiority of Christianity ought not to be construed as, in principle, merely a judgment that proceeds from criteria inherent in his own religious tradition. Nor should Otto's interest in other religions and in the science of religion be seen simply as that of a Christian apologist for whom the science of religion is merely a preliminary to the task of Christian theology. Rather, I hope to show that, for Otto, theology is *Religions-*

wissenschaft, and to the extent that its subject matter (the history and comparison of religions) is drawn from the study of religion itself, *Religionswissenschaft* is theology. Although the approach to these issues and the solutions offered may vary throughout Otto's life, his concern for the autonomy and validity of religion in general, his quest for the criteria of religious truth (both of religion and among religions), and his developing account of the interplay between rational and nonrational elements in religion remain constant.

Life and Work: 1869–1909

Louis Karl Rudolf Otto was born in Peine (Hanover) on September 25, 1869. His father, Wilhelm, was a manufacturer and owned factories in Peine and later in nearby Hildesheim. His mother, Katherine Karoline Henriette *née* Reupke, was eighteen years younger than her husband and was very much responsible for the rearing of Rudolf, the twelfth of thirteen children. In 1880 the family moved to Hildesheim. Otto was enrolled in the *Andreanum*, a grammar school in Hildesheim. His father died shortly afterwards.[17]

The household into which Rudolf Otto was born was very religious. He himself describes its evangelical Lutheran piety as very strict, and as a strong influence on his own religious views from an early age: "I couldn't read any history calmly," he later remarked, "unless I was convinced beforehand that the people in it were also devout and not 'catholic,' or Jews or heathens."[18] Furthermore, the desire to be a pastor had developed from his earliest schools days, and he took an avid interest in everything connected with theology. In 1884 he was confirmed in the evangelical Lutheran church.

Otto and his friends were, however, sufficiently open minded to discuss a variety of religious topics, although he admitted to being disappointed by all his classes in religion. His final school report indicates that in religious instruction, as in other subjects, he was a good but by no means outstanding student.[19] Religion remained, however, "dear to me and valued, and became the more so as a result of the opposition I met with. While still children we argued enthusiastically and quite vehemently about the sonship of God and the creation narratives, about Darwinism and spontaneous generation, and I waited anxiously for the time when I could study all these problems thoroughly."[20]

In 1888, having matriculated, Otto began his studies at the Friedrich-Alexander University in Erlangen. His choice was motivated by his desire to avoid the University of Göttingen for fear of being forced into too liberal a theological position. At Erlangen he hoped to be provided with the means to defend the conservative orthodoxy to which he was committed. However, when he was ready to begin his formal theological studies at Easter 1889, he was faced with a choice: either follow his friends to Göttingen, or remain at Erlangen alone. The summer of 1889 saw him in Göttingen. Although he went intending to refuse to have anything to do with modernizing theological tendencies, there nevertheless began at Göttingen "not only a new phase in my theological perspective, but in my life."[21]

A different Rudolf Otto returned to Erlangen for the winter semester of 1889–90. He was particularly impressed by the systematic theologian Franz Reinhold von Frank, the founder of the Erlangen school of theology. Frank attempted to do justice to both the subjective and objective poles of faith. According to him, the Christian's experience of regeneration is the basis of Christian doctrine; moreover, this experience points beyond itself to its efficient and sustaining cause, namely, God. Otto's own emphasis on the subjective and objective grounds of religion has its roots here. And, most important, it was through Frank that Otto came to know of the work of Schleiermacher. Otto's highly conservative approach to Scripture wavered in the face of

Frank's much more liberal approach, and of his subjectivism in general. Certainly during this second period at Erlangen there occurred a crisis in Otto's theological development which saw him breaking not only with his earlier conservatism, but also with most of his Erlangen teachers. Of the end of his time at Erlangen, he later recalled, "The earth disappeared from under my feet. That was the result of my studies at Erlangen. I went there not so much to quest for truth, but more to vindicate belief. I left with the resolve to seek nothing but the truth, even at the risk of not finding it in Christ."[22]

From late 1889 until early 1891 Otto studied in Bavaria, but in the summer of 1891 he enrolled again at Göttingen, where he remained as a student until 1899. During this period he formed a particular attachment to Theodor Häring, a member of the Ritschlian school. Otto was impressed as much by Häring's personal qualities as by his academic work, and Otto strove to make those qualities his own—carefulness in judgments, empathy for different viewpoints, and respect for those who held them. Otto was to dedicate *Das Heilige* to Häring.

From 1891 to 1898 Otto appears to have distanced himself increasingly both from any narrow confessionalism and from any intimate commitment to the dominant Ritschlian school of theology. He became interested in art, history, music, and architecture, spheres which were to influence his study of religion considerably.[23]

Probably as a consequence of his studies in Aramaic and Arabic, Otto undertook a journey to Egypt, Palestine, and Greece in 1895. In Cairo he encountered Coptic Orthodoxy and was enormously impressed by the aesthetics of the Coptic liturgy. In one of his letters he wrote, "It was as if a piece of the life of the primitive church itself had taken place before my eyes."[24] His first encounter with Islam, in the form of the dervishes, was less promising, for he was appalled by its commercial aspect. But it is important to note that, at the end of his description of the ritual, Otto was already concerned about the possibility of relating such an event to a "systematics of religious feeling."[25] One cannot help but think that this initial experience of Islam molded his attitude toward this tradition in general, for Otto's central criticism of Islam was always that it subordinated the rational elements of religion to the nonrational, and of all religions Otto seems to have had the least empathy for Islam.[26] However that may be, this particular experience does appear to be echoed in his discussion of salvation in Islam in *Das Heilige*:

> Islam, too, embodies the longing for and the experience of salvation. In this case "salvation" is not simply in the "hope" of the joys of Paradise: rather, the most vital element in Islam is "Islam" itself, i.e., that surrender to Allah which is not merely the dedication of the will to him, but also at the same time the entering upon the "Allah" state of mind here and now, the object of longing and striving, a frame of mind which *is* already "salvation," and which may possess and enrapture the man like an intoxication and can give rise to a mystic transport of bliss.[27]

This journey as a whole shows the interest in the praxis of religion which is so characteristic of Otto's work. Throughout the many letters which recount it there is evidence of a highly sensitive appreciation of his surroundings and an empathy for those with whom he came into contact. The events of Holy Week and Easter in Jerusalem left an enormous impression on him, but even more important, during this journey Otto himself had two separate experiences of the grandeur, sublimity, and mystery of the universe.

The first of these experiences occurred while Otto was visiting the Sphinx at Giza. The general feeling of "the unfathomable depth and mystery of existence," he writes, "was most vividly present to the writer, in the evening silence of the sandy desert, that faces the huge Sphinx of Giza and its eyes gazing into the infinite."[28] And while journeying with a group of friends, he has what he regards as a religious experience. As he approaches Jerusalem he experiences most vividly something of the sublimity of nature:

> I had let my friends ride ahead while another section of the party remained further behind me. Evening was coming. We had said goodbye to the gracious old monks of St. John's monastery, the bells of which, echoing as if in greeting, were becoming quieter and quieter, gradually dying away. Now the sun was sinking and the shadows continued to extend over the plain. The long chain and the high peaks of the mountains of Judea loomed before us, sharply outlined in the golden Western sky; to the left, in the distance, lay the surface of the Dead Sea. In the background, however, the mountains of Moab presented an indescribably beautiful sight. Dark and immense masses of clouds had collected over them, illuminated here and there by reflections of the setting sun. There, right next to one of the highest peaks, there begins to emerge a rainbow of wonderful brilliance with the most delicate colors, sparkling more and more and silhouetted against the darkest clouds. And directly next to it, another with the colors inverted, and finally around both of these a third, woven quite finely and delicately. This sparkles until the sun is quite gone, and then it fades away slowly and disappears. In front of us, however, towards the West, the vault of Heaven is wonderfully blue and infinitely deep for a long time, until, growing dark, out of its depths the stars light up. At such moments, the fragmented self is integrated and becomes aware of its place within the whole.[29]

This passage reflects quite clearly the romantic vision of nature; Schleiermacher's notion of the intuition of the infinite in the finite and the eternal in the temporal is analogous to it. There are intimations here also of the close connection which Otto makes in his later writings between the experience of the sublime in nature and the experience of the sacred.[30]

Later, after his return to Göttingen, Otto completed his first major work, "Geist und Wort nach Luther" ("Spirit and Word According to Luther"). For it he received the degree of Licentiate of Theology, and the study was published in the same year, 1898, under the title *Die Anschauung vom heiligen Geiste bei Luther* (*Luther's Conception of the Holy Spirit*).[31] Since Otto was nurtured in Lutheranism and schooled in Lutheran theology, it is not surprising that Luther's own thought, and more especially his own experience, had a significant influence on him. And that influence was not merely one sided, for Otto would often appeal to Luther for validation of or support for his own views, and in so doing would offer significantly fresh interpretations of the nature and context of Luther's work. Moreover, the concept of "Spirit" developed in this work was to play some role not only in *The Idea of the Holy*, but also in Otto's later understanding of mysticism and of primitive Christian eschatology.

In 1899 Otto was made a *Privatdozent* in the University of Göttingen, and until 1904 his work proceeded in a number of different though related directions. Schleiermacher's *Speeches on Religion*,[32] newly edited by Otto, appeared in 1899, followed in 1903 by an essay on Schleiermacher's rediscovery of the essence of religion.[33] This latter was preceded in 1901 by *Leben und Wirken Jesu*,[34] a work which stands firmly within the tradition established by Immanuel Kant's *Religion within the Limits of Reason Alone* and developed in the nineteenth-century quest for an authentic life of the historical Jesus. Of all of Otto's works, this one most clearly bears the stamp of the Ritschlian theology. It was especially as a result of this work, and more generally as a consequence of his liberal theological approach, that Otto was excluded from a full professorial position by the Lutheran church. Only when this veto was removed by the church authorities was his position as a full professor made possible, at Breslau in 1915. During the later part of his time as a *Privatdozent*, Otto considered abandoning theology and contemplated becoming a pastor at a German church in Paris or a missionary in China.[35] He came close to a nervous breakdown, but he remained a theologian, at least partly as a consequence of the encouragement and support he received from Ernst Troeltsch. In reply to a letter in which Otto had asked to be allowed to visit him in order to discuss his future, Troeltsch wrote, "You must now, above all, pull yourself together, and call to mind the views which you hold for yourself as a man, quite apart from any and every theology. You must have views which are for your own personal use. What you do with theology, we will want to look further into. . . . If it doesn't go well, then you will just have to begin something different. For the moment, attend in general only to peace of mind and the strength of the inner man."[36]

Otto was to take up the problem of Jesus again only late in his career. He significantly revised his earlier views of primitive Christianity in his last major work, *Reich Gottes und Menschensohn*.[37] His early work on Jesus was followed in 1904 by *Naturalistische und religiöse Weltansicht*,[38] in which Otto attempts to establish the autonomy of religion from the natural sciences from the position of Kant's transcendental idealism, although his philosophical commitment remains incipient at this time. In this same year he was appointed an associate professor at Göttingen, a position he held until 1914.

During the early part of his time in this position at Göttingen Otto found that philosophy which was to provide the key to the understanding of religion for him—the Kantianism of Jakob Fries. Friesianism was undergoing something of a renaissance at Göttingen during this time, as was Kantianism in other parts of Germany, due in the main to the able leadership of Leonard Nelson. He and a number of like-minded colleagues went to some lengths to convert Otto to the neo-Friesian viewpoint.[39] Out of his newfound Friesian conviction there appeared in 1909 what was to become a standard textbook of this movement, *Kantisch-Fries'sche Religionsphilosophie*.[40] While there is some later development in Otto's ideas beyond the Friesian position, he seems never to have rejected it, although it becomes progressively more implied than stated. Throughout his career he saw it as the proper philosophical foundation of the science of religion.[41]

Life and Work: 1910–37

Throughout 1911 and 1912 Otto was traveling extensively, first to Tenerife and North Africa, subsequently to India and the Far East. The first journey, which began in March, 1911, is of no little significance, for during it Otto came to recognize the central place of "the Holy" in religion. This journey is customarily seen, quite properly, as providing the origin of those ideas which were to come to fruition in *Das Heilige*. Otto's conviction of the centrality of "the Holy" was aroused by an experience of synagogue worship at Mogador (now Essaouria) in Morocco. As he described it in one of his travel letters,

> It is Sabbath, and already in the dark and inconceivably grimy passage of the house we hear that sing-song of prayers and reading of scripture, that nasal half-singing half-speaking sound which Church and Mosque have taken over from the Synagogue. The sound is pleasant, one can soon distinguish certain modulations and cadences that follow one another at regular intervals like *Leitmotive*. The ear tries to grasp individual words but it is scarcely possible and one has almost given up the attempt when suddenly out of the babel of voices, causing a thrill of fear, there it

begins, unified, clear and unmistakable: *Kadosh,
Kadosh, Kadosh Elohim Adonai Zebaoth Male'u
hashamayim wahaarets kebodo!* (Holy, Holy, Holy,
Lord God of Hosts, the heavens and the earth are full
of thy glory).

I have heard the *Sanctus Sanctus Sanctus* of the
cardinals in St. Peter's, the *Swiat Swiat Swiat* in the
Cathedral of the Kremlin and the Holy Holy Holy of
the Patriarch in Jerusalem. In whatever language they
resound, these most exalted words that have ever
come from human lips always grip one in the depths
of the soul, with a mighty shudder exciting and call-
ing into play the mystery of the other world latent
therein. And this more than anywhere else here in
this modest place, where they resound in the same
tongue in which Isaiah first received them and from
the lips of the people whose first inheritance they
were.[42]

Whether this journey saw the birth of those ideas which
were to reach their full development in Otto's later works,
or whether ideas forming in his mind were brought to full
consciousness as a result of the trip is difficult to determine precisely. Certainly their outlines are already evident
in Otto's review of Wilhelm Wundt's *Völkerpsychologie*.[43]
But undoubtedly the journey to North Africa, and shortly
after to Asia, gave Otto's subsequent writings a breadth and
depth beyond that of virtually all of his contemporaries in
the comparative study of religions. From this time on, his
work gives as much the impression of a *Religionswissenschaftler* as of a Lutheran theologian or idealist philosopher.

In October, 1911, Otto began a journey which was to last
until the end of July. He first visited India, where he came
into contact with Muslims, Hindus, Sikhs, and Parsees. In
Rangoon he encountered Burmese Buddhism, of which he
remarks, perhaps a little naively, "Buddhism has been pre-
served here in a very pure form and appears very viable."[44]

Otto's letters indicate that he was impressed by the Theravada traditions of Burma and Thailand, but more so by Japanese Zen Buddhism. In fact, he was the first German scholar of religion to visit Zen monasteries, to converse with Zen masters, and to be introduced by them into the practice of Zen meditation. This personal experience enabled him later to see such meditation as a means of experiencing the nonrational essence of the Holy.[45] While in Japan he lectured to a large assembly of Zen monks on parallels between Christianity and Buddhism, and to the Asiatic Society of Japan.[46] After a stay of some two months in China, during which he familiarized himself with Taoism, Otto returned to Germany via the Trans-Siberian Railway and Moscow.

This journey was important for the development of Otto's career in a number of other ways. First, during this trip Otto first formed the idea for a collection of the cultic and ritual means of religious expression.[47] Neither in Göttingen nor in Breslau was it possible for him to realize his plan. Not until 1926, in Marburg, was he able to found the collection with a capital grant of some three thousand marks. In 1927 it was firmly established through government assistance, and a further grant of some forty thousand marks was allocated for the purchase of appropriate religious objects. On his journey to Asia from October, 1927, to May, 1928, Otto used part of the funds to acquire Egyptian, Buddhist, and especially Hindu cultic and aesthetic objects.[48]

Second, it was probably during this journey that Otto conceived the idea of a League of Religions. A paper which he delivered in 1913 to the World Congress for Free Christianity and Religious Progress in Paris already contains the theoretical framework for such a league. In it he argues that, in spite of the "diversity of spirits," religions are nonetheless united in their fight against irreligion and superstition and therefore in the necessity of guaranteeing the survival of true religion:

If we are to ensure that the strong, pure, eternal spiritual content of religion itself in its truth and sincerity, mature in a genuine modernity, shall subsist side by side with modern ways of thinking, we have to undertake the great task, universal in its application, of a purifying criticism which will modernize religion, bringing out its ideals, and will eliminate the accretions which have attached to it in the course of historical development, together with all mythical and legendary irrelevancies and attitudes to history and the universe which are not reconcilable with the truth. This is a task which inevitably transcends the bounds of one's own religion, and in which one turns instinctively to establish contact with others, working on similar lines.[49]

Not until February, 1920, did Otto begin to work in earnest on the establishment of such a league,[50] but from that time until around 1924 he devoted an enormous amount of effort to it.

The first formal meeting of the "religioser Menschheitsbund" was held on August 1, 1922, at Wilhelmshagen (near Berlin), with representatives from eight different religious and confessional groups present.[51] During this meeting Otto reportedly said, "In this work of renewal [of cooperation between nations] the religions must assume the leadership. A religious community must also out of inner necessity be a moral working-group, it has great moral responsibilities to fulfill among all humanity if it does not wish to fall prey to meaninglessness."[52] And the League *was* intended primarily as a forum for the discussion of pressing moral issues of international significance. It reflected Otto's own emphasis on the importance of the rational (that is, moral elements in religion) and Otto's own belief in the autonomous and universal validity of the moral imperative—that it was, so to speak, independent from culture. In a quite unsympathetic social and cultural context the basic program of the League propounded an almost naive and simplistic optimism regarding the rational and moral possibilities inherent in human nature, an attitude more redolent of the nineteenth century than of the third decade of the twentieth.

To be sure, there appears to have been an enthusiastic initial response to the organization. In 1922 the membership lists include 470 people, a good proportion of whom were members of non-Christian traditions.[53] After 1924, though, the impetus appears to have lessened, and by 1933 the League, much like its political counterpart, had ceased to be active.[54]

The third result of Otto's journeys was his much deeper subsequent involvement in the study of world religions. Otto's library borrowings from late 1912 to 1915 suggest that he was reading voraciously about Hinduism and Buddhism.[55] Shortly after his return from India, he conceived a plan to bring out a series of German translations of the most important sacred texts of the world religions. January, 1913, saw him writing to the finance minister in Berlin seeking support for this project,[56] and in May, 1914, Otto pressed his claims for financial support in the Prussian Parliament, where he served as a member from 1913 to 1918.[57] As a result of Otto's efforts Hermann Oldenburg was appointed president of a commission established to bring out this series under the title *Quellen der Religionsgeschichte* (Sources of the History of Religion), and Otto served as one of its two principal secretaries.

Unfortunately, we do not know when Otto came to learn Sanskrit. Friedrich Heiler suggests, probably rightly, that he began to study it while in the Himalayas.[58] If we assume it took about four years for him to gain sufficient competence to produce creditable translations, then Otto must have begun at or shortly after this time, since in 1916 he published his first translation of a Sanskrit text, namely *Dīpikā des Nivāsa*,[59] followed in 1917 by *Vischnu-Nārāyana*[60] and *Siddhānta des Rāmānuja*.[61]

In Otto's later years there appeared a new translation of the whole *Bhagavad-Gītā* under the title *Der Sang des Hehr-Erhabenen* (*The Song of the Supremely Exalted One*).[62] Otto also published in 1934 a textual analysis of the *Bhagavad-Gītā* with a view to discerning its primitive form,[63] and 1935 saw the appearance of *Die Lehr-Traktate der Bhagavad-Gītā*.[64] Otto's translations saw their completion in 1936 with that of the *Katha Upanishad*.[65] In all of these translations Otto was concerned not only with the philological elucidation of the texts, but also (and perhaps even more so) with the understanding of the religious experience expressed through them. Perhaps for this reason Otto's translations were not overenthusiastically received by German Indologists, who thought them on the whole to be too loose.[66]

In 1917, the year of publication of *Das Heilige*,[67] Otto took up a chair in Systematic Theology at the University of Marburg, where he succeeded the Ritschlian theologian Wilhelm Herrmann. As noted earlier, he was to remain there until his retirement in 1929. In 1923 he was invited to deliver the Haskell lectures at Oberlin College in the United States. He took as his theme the comparison of Eastern and Western mysticism, and from these lectures arose his comparison of Meister Eckhart and Shankara, *West-östliche Mystik*.[68] In the foreword to this volume Otto points to the significance of his time spent in India for his understanding of the differences between Western and Eastern religious traditions: "Here for the first time in actuality I saw opening out before me the curious parallels between the feeling and experience of the Eastern and Western worlds. But I also recognized their intimate peculiarities and dissimilarities."[69]

These convergences and divergences between Christianity and Hinduism were further explored in *Die Gnadenreligion Indiens und das Christentum*,[70] an expanded version of his Olaus Petri lectures delivered at Uppsala in 1927,[71] while 1932 saw the publication of *Gottheit und Gottheiten*

der Arier (*Deity and Deities of the Aryans*).[72] In the same
year there appeared a collection of essays illustrating the
numinous experience by examples drawn from the history
of religions under the title *Das Gefühl des Überweltlichen*
(*The Feeling of the Supra-mundane*),[73] and a more theologically oriented collection entitled *Sünde und Urschuld* (*Sin
and Original Guilt*).[74] Both of these volumes of collected
essays arose from the progressively increasing number of
appendices to *Das Heilige*, some of which were first published in a separate volume in 1923 as *Aufsätze das Numinose betreffend* (*Essays concerning the Numinous*).[75]

From October 18, 1927, until May 14, 1928, Otto was
once again traveling in the East—Ceylon, India, Palestine,
Asia Minor, and the Balkans. The trip is of interest for two
reasons. First, Otto again has an experience of the sacred,
during a three-day stay on Elephanta island near Bombay:

> One climbs halfway up the mountainside on magnifi-
> cent stone steps until a wide gate opens on the right,
> in the volcanic rocks. This leads into one of the
> mightiest of early Indian rock temples. Heavy pillars
> hewn out of the rock support the roof. The eye slowly
> accustoms itself to the semi-darkness, gradually dis-
> tinguishes awesome representations—carved into the
> wall—of the religious epics of India, until it reaches
> the imposing central recess. Here an image rises up
> out of the rock which I can only compare with a few
> of the sculptures of Japan and with the great represen-
> tations of Christ in early Byzantine churches. It is a
> three-headed form, carved only as far as the breast . . .
> in threefold human size. . . . Still and powerful the
> central head looks down, with both the others in pro-
> file. Over the image rests a perfect peace and majesty.
> Shiva is represented here as the one who creates, pre-
> serves, and destroys the world, and yet as the one who
> also saves and blesses. Nowhere else have I found the
> secret of the transcendent, the other world more

> grandly and perfectly expressed than in these three
> heads. . . . To see this place were alone worth a journey
> to India, while from the spirit of religion which has
> lived here, one may experience more in a single hour
> of contemplation than from all the books.[76]

Second, this trip may well have reaffirmed Otto's conviction that the specific differences between Christianity and
Hinduism were a function not of their nonrational core, but
of their respective ethical development. And certainly the
relationship between ethics and religion was at the center of
Otto's later writings. In five articles written in 1931 and
1932, he attempted to justify the absolute objective value
found in religion.[77] He had planned to develop this theme
in the Gifford lectures, which he was invited to give in
1933, under the title "Moral Law and the Will of God." (His
increasingly ill health unfortunately obliged him to forego
the presentation of these lectures.) The direction in which
his thinking was moving is also indicated in a volume on
freedom and necessity upon which he was working at the
time of his death, and which was eventually edited by
Theodor Siegfried and published.[78]

Otto died on March 6, 1937,[79] aged sixty-seven, in somewhat tragic and mysterious circumstances. The immediate
cause of his death was pneumonia which he contracted
some eight days after entering the psychiatric hospital in
Marburg. Allied to this was severe arteriosclerosis which
was subsequently shown to have begun twenty years before.

Otto had entered the psychiatric hospital in order to overcome morphine addiction. He had been treated with morphine in order to alleviate the pain resulting from an accident five months before.[80] In early October, 1936, Otto had
hiked—alone, uncharacteristically—to Staufenberg, near
Marburg. After making a strenuous climb to the top of a
manor-house tower, he fell some sixty feet.

The causes of this event are unclear, but I believe the
evidence points to a suicide attempt. The injuries that Otto

received—a broken leg and broken foot—do not necessarily show that he had either accidentally fallen, or as has been suggested, suffered a heart attack.[81] Moreover, while it was not impossible for one to fall from the tower, it was nonetheless highly improbable.

Otto had been subject to periods of deep depression throughout his life.[82] He was depressed at the time of the fall and remained so afterward. In December, 1936, his sister, Johanne Ottmer, wrote to his close friend Birger Forell, "Rudolf complains much about his head, so that he cannot often think coherently; also depressions have set in again. . . . He cries more often."[83] While in the psychiatric hospital, Otto tried to leave in order to throw himself under a train,[84] as his close Jewish friend Hermann Jacobsohn had done in April, 1933, for fear of being placed in a concentration camp.[85]

Throughout 1936, Otto was increasingly concerned about his failing health. In late April he wrote to Forell, "I have had a bad attack of influenza for ten weeks and was so weak that I could scarcely function. I can still do no work and lie down almost the whole day."[86] His distress is evident in another letter to Forell, written on May 31: "We have been having a very difficult time. Johanne had an accident in March, I myself was so ill for a quarter of a year through influenza that I didn't know what was going to come of it."[87] The lack of certainty about what happened at Staufenberg speaks most decisively against the suggestion that it was an accident, for, had it been, one might expect those closest to him to have been aware of that. We can only presume that Otto failed to tell anyone what happened, and in none of his subsequent correspondence is there any account of the event.

Otto was buried in the Marburg Friedhof with the inscription "Heilig, Heilig, Heilig, ist der Herr Zabaoth."

2
The Context of Otto's Thought

The Rational and the Nonrational

In Otto's mature philosophy, religions are viewed as consisting of both rational and nonrational elements. While religions have to do with theoretical and moral ideas, they are not finally dependent on these. Rather, these rational components are ultimately referrable to an object or "subject" that can only be apprehended in a nonrational "unique original feeling-response"[1] that is the core of all religions. Otto, standing squarely within the nineteenth-century tradition of the quest for the essence of religion, finds it partly in a nonrational core, and this is constituted by a specific and unique kind of experience: the numinous experience. We shall return to what Otto means by "nonrational," "original feeling-response," "numinous," and so on. For the moment, it suffices to note that the clarification of the core of religion, and of its connection to religion's rational factors, is the overall aim of *Das Heilige*, and indeed, of Otto's work as a whole.[2]

Those who see Otto as an irrationalist are mistaken for two reasons. First, he certainly recognizes the place and validity of rational thought in religion, but (and this is crucial) *only* insofar as this is related to religion's nonrational core, and insofar as this is recognized as deriving from it. For example: "we count this the very mark and criterion of a religion's high rank and superior value—that it should have no lack of *conceptions* about God; that it should admit knowledge—the knowledge that comes by faith—of the transcendent in terms of conceptual thought."[3] The harmony between rational and nonrational factors in religions is the central means by which their relative rank may be determined.

Second, for Otto, the rational defense of religion is a necessary prelude to any consideration of its nonrational essence. In the foreword to the English edition of *Das Heilige* he remarks, with reference to his *Naturalism and Religion* and *The Philosophy of Religion*, "And I feel that no one ought to concern himself with the 'Numen ineffabile' who has not already devoted assiduous and serious study to the 'Ratio aeterna.'"[4] Already in 1909, foreshadowing his work yet to come, Otto points out that the focus for a science of religion is religious experience, *and* that the philosophy of Jakob Fries is the key to its interpretation: "Our foundation in the philosophy of religion gives us a general method of interpreting this strange phenomenon, the true center of religious experience: it is the obscure knowledge of the Eternal in general and of the eternal determination of Existence, which comes to life in feeling."[5]

In short, the rational is by no means despised by Otto. The rational elements within religion are seen as significant; also, the relations of its rational and nonrational elements (and therefore religion as a whole) are illuminated by a rational metaphysical system, albeit one with an important place reserved for feeling.

Even at this point it is worth forewarning the reader that Otto's attempt to do justice to both elements in religion is a complex one, and his determination of the nature of religion in terms of a rational metaphysics is problematic. Be that as it may, Otto's attempt to effect a viable synthesis of these factors clearly arises from the various theological and philosophical influences upon this development. My primary concern in this chapter is to clarify these. Whether Otto effectively synthesizes a multiplicity of diverse currents or merely reflects willy-nilly the various spirits of his time is a question whose answer can only be broached at the conclusion of this study. Did he, *could* he, weld into a whole the concerns of those movements and individuals from which he derived his materials? This question must be kept in mind as we proceed.

The Nonrational in Christian History

Otto certainly does not claim that his emphasis on the nonrational core of religion is original. Rather, he sees himself as part of a tradition which has stressed the nonrational since the beginning of Christianity, although he recognizes that this is a constant yet always threatened tradition. According to Otto, Christianity (and other religions) developed a continuing bias toward rationalization and intellectualization at the expense of the nonrational core. Orthodox Christianity, for example, in its failure to recognize the value of the nonrational, "gave to the idea of God a one-sidedly intellectualistic and rationalistic interpretation."[6] This bias occurs not only in Catholicism from the time of the great medieval scholastics, but also in Protestantism from the time of the Lutheran scholastic Johann Gerhardt (1582–1637) onward.[7]

For Otto, this interplay—even conflict—between rational and nonrational elements in religion has shown itself throughout Christian history: in the conflict between the God of the philosophers and the biblical God; in the contest between the Stoic idea of the divine impassibility and Lactantius's assertion of the incomprehensibility, majesty, and wrath of God; in Duns Scotus's emphasis on love and the will, as opposed to the Thomist stress on knowledge and reason. But it is above all in the Platonic tradition as a whole, mediated through Chrysostom, Gregory of Nyssa, Plotinus, Augustine, Pseudo-Dionysius, and Meister Eckhart, that Otto sees the continuity of tradition insuring the survival of the nonrational, at least until the time of the eighteenth-century Enlightenment. This continuity of tradition is, for Otto, grounded in Plato, who "grasps the object of religion by quite different means than those of conceptual thinking, viz. by the 'ideograms' of myth, by 'enthusiasm' or inspiration, 'eros' or love, 'mania' or the divine frenzy. He abandons the attempt to bring the object of religion into one system of knowledge with the objects of 'science' (ἐπιστημη), i.e., reason, and it becomes something not less but greater thereby."[8]

Otto finds the nonrational essence of religion reflected especially in the life and writings of Martin Luther. If we take Otto at his word, his work on Luther brought him to a recognition of the nonrational in religion and enabled him to see Luther as part of a tradition reaching back through the German mystics[9] to the neo-Platonists and to Plato himself: "Indeed, I grew to understand the numinous and its difference from the rational in Luther's *De Servo Arbitrio* long before I identified it in the *qādôsh* of the Old Testament and in the elements of 'religious awe' in the history of religion in general."[10] Evidence for this claim can certainly be found in Otto's work on Luther, *Die Anschauung vom heiligen Geiste bei Luther*. If the substantive conclusions of Otto's later works are only to be found in embryonic form here, the framework of much of his later work is nevertheless substantially in evidence. First, in spite of the Ritschlian flavor of the work, it goes beyond Ritschlianism in its assertion of the essentially nonrational depths of religion, and in its view of "Spirit" in Luther as the "bearer and creator of *religious* capacities."[11] Thus there is already in this work a clear sense of the autonomy of religion. Moreover, there is a recognition of a specific type of experience that is of its essence religious in nature,[12] and, allied with this, the claim that such experience points beyond itself to its object and is therefore in itself "experience of the grace of God."[13] That the study of religion and theology needs to be grounded in analysis of the religious consciousness—the pivotal issue in Otto's theory of religion—

has its origin in this, Otto's first work: "The religious feeling has rightful claim to its own scope, unimpaired and unobstructed. It should not allow itself to be curtailed or eliminated in favor of other plausible trains of thought; and it may well be the task of theology to reexamine that crushing chain of empirical relationships until it can find place for an answer to the question how religion is possible—and possible, moreover, in uncurtailed form."[14]

Otto wants to maintain that, despite Luther's own experience and despite emphasis on the nonrational, this numinous depth was lost in later Lutheranism: "More and more it deprived the forms of worship of the genuinely contemplative and specifically 'devotional' elements in them. The conceptual and doctrinal—the ideal of orthodoxy—began to preponderate over the inexpressible, whose only life is in the conscious mental attitude of the devout soul."[15] This is not to say that the nonrational aspect of Christianity was extinguished after the Reformation. Rather, it continued alongside and in interplay with its rationalist alternative, making its presence felt in both Catholicism and Protestantism, particularly in their more mystical expressions.

Protestant nonrationalism in the period between the Reformation and the Enlightenment is exemplified for Otto in a number of individuals, all of whom were in conflict with the orthodoxy of their respective times and who therefore were more in tune with the inner spirit of Luther's teaching. Despite the rationalism of his theosophy, Otto maintains that in the Protestant mystic Jakob Böhme (1575–1624), for example, "The consciousness of the numinous was astir and alive as an element of genuine value: so that herein Böhme was an heir of Luther, preserving what in Luther's own school came to be overlooked and disregarded."[16] Mention is also made of the Lutheran theologian and mystical writer Johann Arndt (1555–1621), of the theologian and translator of mystical texts Gottfried Arnold (1666–97), and of Philipp Jakob Spener (1635–1705), the founder of Pietism. Undoubtedly what Otto found attractive in all of these men was their "pietistic" stance. Their attention was focussed on the *felt* character of religion, on inner conviction, on intensity of feeling; on the affective and the emotional elements of religion, as opposed to the vacuous rationalism of an intellectualist orthodoxy.

It is consequently somewhat surprising that, in *Das Heilige*, no mention is made of Count Nicholas von Zinzendorf (1700–1760), the leader of the Moravian Pietists at Herrnhut in Saxony. The count is only mentioned twice in any of Otto's previously published works, specifically in the epilogue to his edition of Schleiermacher's *Speeches on Religion*. Zinzendorf is a central figure in the history of pietistic movements, as Albrecht Ritschl made clear in the third volume of his *History of Pietism* (1886).[17] Although Otto was aware of the connection between Schleiermacher and Moravian Pietism as early as 1899,[18] and of the fact that Fries was brought up as a Moravian Pietist by 1908,[19] he seems not to have realized the importance of Zinzendorf both for his own theory of religion and for the influence upon Schleiermacher until much later.[20]

In 1919 an article appeared which (for Otto, at any rate) threw new light on Zinzendorf's account of religion.[21] It was especially concerned to present an address to be given by Zinzendorf to a synod of his community in 1745, and it prompted Otto to produce a paper entitled "Zinzendorf über den 'Sensus numinis.' "[22] In this article Otto points to intimations of his own account of religion in several aspects of Zinzendorf's writing. Zinzendorf sees *Scheu* (dread) and *Entsetzen* (horror) as uniquely determinative of religious feeling, affections which are quite analogous to Otto's delineation of the moment of *tremendum* in numinous experience. In addition, in Zinzendorf's use and explanation of the term *sensus numinis* Otto finds a close parallel to his own view. The relevant passage from Zinzendorf is as follows: "What is given above is simply to prove that in all human creatures there is a Sensus Numinis which indeed lies often very deep, but which the smallest contact from outside makes sensible to the subject himself and palpable to him who experiences it."[23]

This discovery of Zinzendorf later led Otto to see Schleiermacher as much more heavily dependent on Moravian Pietism than he had previously thought. In a revised version of his earlier paper on Zinzendorf, significantly retitled "Zinzendorf as Discoverer of the Sensus Numinis,"[24] Otto remarks that Zinzendorf was concerned not with dogmatics or theology, but with the essence of all religion: "It is an attempt at . . . as we would say, a 'phenomenology of religion' which seeks for the basic and essential moments of religious feeling, and is to this extent a forerunner of the writings of another 'Herrnhuter,' namely Schleiermacher, and of his *Speeches on Religion* and the introductory sections of his later *The Christian Faith*."[25] Otto further maintains that the origin of Schleiermacher's use of the term *Gefühl* (feeling) may be seen in this address, and that the notion of *Ahndung* is used in the same sense by Zinzendorf as by Schleiermacher and, more especially, by Fries:

> The connection which Schleiermacher later sets up in his second and fifth *Speeches on Religion* between general experience of the transcendent and the Christian idea of redemption, and then in the introduction to his *The Christian Faith* between the general feeling of dependence (an obvious transformation of the general *sensus numinis*) and religious feelings of Christian determination, is so similar to these assertions of Zinzendorf that one would like to posit a direct line of transmission between these two *Herrnhuter*.[26]

Early in his career, when he was most inclined to see Schleiermacher as the savior of modern theology, Otto did overstress the intellectualism and rationalism of eighteenth-century cultural life and consequently tended to ignore those powerful pietistic currents which were also present. Indeed, he went so far as to imply that Pietism was virtually nonexistent in the eighteenth century.[27] For Otto, the philosophy of the Enlightenment was intensely one sided: "It valued man essentially as a being thinking according to the laws of intelligence and acting according to the laws of morality, as the creature of 'theoretic' and 'practical' reason. It was blind to that wealth of human nature which lies outside the scope of these capacities, to the rich profundities of immediate experience of life, and nature, and history, which lie beyond rationalistic analysis and moralistic considerations."[28] Of the enlightened person's attitude toward religion he writes: "One did not hate religion but one somehow held it in contempt like something for which one no longer had any use. One was cultured and full of ideals; one was aesthetic, and one was moral, but one was no longer religious."[29]

This is not to be taken as suggesting that religion was under any sort of virulent attack in eighteenth-century Germany. German thought had resisted the onslaught of French materialism and atheism, as exemplified for Otto in d'Holbach (1723–89) and De la Mettrie (1705–51).[30] Indeed, the Enlightenment, says Otto, "prided itself on having overcome 'atheism,'"[31] although only by the subjection of religion to rational criticism. Still, the *sensus numinis* had been lost, and religion's "essential spirit which, as any pious person feels, is something quite different from the intellectual perception of some metaphysical things or the observance of ordinances, had escaped."[32]

Otto was subsequently to see the Enlightenment in a somewhat more positive light. But considering the above-quoted kind of judgment of it, and his underplaying of the Pietistic tradition of the period, it is clear why Schleiermacher could appear to the early Otto as the revitalizer of the nonrational Christian tradition that had, in Otto's view, been dormant for most of the eighteenth century. Schleiermacher, according to Otto, "opened for his age a new door to old and forgotten ideas: to divine marvel instead of supernatural miracle, to living revelation instead of instilled doctrine, to the manifestation of the divinely infinite in event, person, and history, and especially to a new understanding and valuation of biblical history as divine revelation."[33]

The Kantian Connection

Before considering the significance of Schleiermacher for nineteenth-century religious thought, and for Otto, it is necessary to give a brief account of the philosophy of Immanuel Kant (1724–1804). Neither Schleiermacher nor Fries nor Otto can be understood apart from his relation to Kantianism. In 1781 the first of Kant's three critiques, the *Critique of Pure Reason*, appeared. While epitomizing eighteenth-century thought, it signaled the beginning of a new era in philosophy. As Karl Barth has aptly put it, "It was in this man and in this work that the eighteenth century saw, understood and affirmed itself in its own limitations. Itself—in its limitations."[34] The validity of this statement derives from Kant's unique blending of two separate streams of eighteenth-century thought—rationalism and empiricism—in his attempt to subject reason itself to rational criticism.[35]

Steeped in the rationalist tradition mediated to him from Leibniz via his teacher Christian Wolff, Kant nonetheless rejected the rationalist claim that pure thinking could generate knowledge of absolute reality. Having been awoken from his dogmatic slumbers (as he rather rhetorically put it) by the empiricism of David Hume, he asserted that knowledge had to be related to the tough givenness of experience. Theoretical knowledge is thereby limited to the phenomenal realm (the realm of things as they appear to us) and does not extend to the noumenal realm (the realm of the "thing-in-itself"). God, freedom, and immortality are by definition "parts" of the noumenal realm and are not possible objects of theoretical knowledge.

Still, Kant remains sufficiently wedded to rationalism to maintain that empiricism is misguided in supposing that *all* knowledge derives from experience, even if it originates there. "For it may well be," he writes, "that our empirical knowledge is made up of what we receive through impressions and of what our own faculty of knowledge (sensible impressions serving merely as the occasion) supplies from itself."[36] Moreover, if all knowledge were dependent on experience alone, there could be no certain knowledge; because experience can only give us generalizations from fact, these are always open to the possibility of refutation in the next moment by a contrary experience. What is learned from experience alone, therefore, does not bear the hallmarks of certain knowledge, namely, *universality* and *necessity*.

Kant's central aim is to show that we do have a priori (that is, universal and necessary) knowledge of things and, further, that such knowledge can only be explained if the character of things as known is determined by the way in which our minds know them. This means that we can never know things as they really are. Rather, we only know things as they appear to us by virtue of the constitutive and determinative powers of our minds.

In that section of the first *Critique* entitled "Transcendental Aesthetic," Kant argues that space and time are not conceptions that can be dependent on experience for their origin. Our intuitions of space and time are a priori because they are the universal and necessary conditions of the possibility of experience. That is to say, insofar as any object is given directly to us in experience, it will be in a spatiotemporal form. As a consequence, space and time are transcendentally ideal—they cannot be supposed to exist independently of our perceptions. They are merely the a priori forms of intuiting what is given to experience through the manifold of sense.

In "Transcendental Analytic," Kant argues that conceptual a prioris match the perceptual ones of space and time. As the "Aesthetic" gave us the pure intuitions of space and time, so the "Analytic" is intended to give us pure concepts or categories under which any and every possible object of knowledge must necessarily be thought.

In Kant's view, we possess one intellectual faculty which has a twofold task: a general task in logic, and a more specific one in making judgments about objects. Kant reasons that, if we want to discover pure concepts or categories of understanding, we can do so by derivation from the concepts of general logic, specifically, the forms of judgment. Because the forms of judgment are the universal and necessary modes of thinking, any and every object of experience can *only* be thought under *all* these necessary and universal forms of judgment. Hence the forms of judgment are necessarily the source of the pure categories of the understanding. In a passage popularly known as the Metaphysical Deduction of the Categories, Kant lists the various forms of judgment under four headings, each containing three divisions and a corresponding list of categories. The categories under the heading *quantity* are unity, plurality, totality; under the head *quality*, reality, negation, limitation; under the head *relation*, subsistence and inherence (*substantia* and *accidens*), causality and dependence (cause and effect), community (interaction between agent and patient); and finally, under the heading *modality*, possibility and impossibility, being and not-being, necessity and contingency. Of these, the most important for Fries, and for Otto, are those under the heading *relation*.

It is crucial to our later discussion that we now take up the distinction between pure and schematized categories. A pure category may be defined as the concept of a particular form of judgment which is able to characterize all things without exception. H. J. Paton points out that "Kant never varies . . . in his belief that the pure categories when we abstract from all reference to time and space, must be regarded as concepts, not of an *object* in general, but of a *thing* in general, that is, of things as they are in themselves. Indeed, so far as we can think of things-in-themselves at all, we must do so by means of the pure categories, for all thinking contains the forms of judgement."[37] But for Kant, the categories can only *legitimately* be applied to the extent that they can be, so to say, cashed in in terms of sense experiences (which have been brought under the a priori forms of intuition). That is, the categories have objective validity only when they are *schematized*, interpreted under the form of time (and space). The categories listed above refer to the categories *as schematized*, not to the pure categories. Indeed, although Kant believes that the pure categories are obtained when time (and space) are abstracted from the categories thus schematized, they cannot really be defined, since they contain no clear property by means of which the object to which they refer can be recognized. "The pure concepts," writes Kant, "can find no object and so can acquire no meaning which might yield a concept of some object."[38] As we shall see, in contrast to Kant, Jakob Fries attempts to derive knowledge of absolute reality by removing the temporal schema. Otto, in his account of the rational side of the Holy, is dependent on the Friesian method.

According to the *Critique of Pure Reason*, the world of actual and possible experience can be known by combining a priori elements contributed by the mind with sense experiences. Space and time do not characterize the noumenal realm and are only applicable to the realm of appearances. The categories of understanding, too, in their schematized form, are only applicable to the phenomenal world. The noumenal realm is outside the bounds of possible knowledge, and those ideas essential to religion—God, freedom, and immortality—are beyond possible knowledge, although within the bounds of faith.

Kant had not said all he wanted to say about reason in the first *Critique*, for reason has also to do with responsible human action. According to the *Critique of Practical Reason*, persons are bound, insofar as they are rational beings, by the moral law—by the necessity of acting out of reverence for lawfulness in general, by the categorical imperative to act only on that maxim through which it can at the same time be willed that it should become a universal law, and by the will for the highest good.

The necessity laid upon us by virtue of our practical reason has, according to Kant, a number of necessary consequences. First, the rational obligation to act morally implies that we *can* do so. Freedom is a universal and necessary precondition of morality, and its reality must consequently be postulated, albeit as pertaining to our actions noumenally and not phenomenally. (Phenomenally, all our actions are causally determined.) Second, the will for the highest good—the conjunction of moral perfection and complete happiness—requires two further postulates of practical reason: the immortality of the soul to provide the necessary time for the self to approach the highest good, and the existence of God to bring about the necessary relationship between virtue and happiness, duty and desire. In the Kantian scheme God is demoted from his position as an object of knowledge but reinstated as a reasonable postulate of practical faith. The obligation that man ought to act so as to achieve the highest good is an obligation conceivable only on the presupposition that God exists.

Schleiermacher and Feeling

This then was the situation when, in 1799, Friedrich Schleiermacher (1772–1834) published his *Speeches on Religion* at the behest of the young Romantic circle with which he had become intimately involved a few years previously. Schleiermacher makes it quite clear that he, like the cultured despisers of religion to whom he writes, scorns the God of speculative reason deposed by the Kantian critique and the ethically dependent Kantian deity. For Schleiermacher, "belief must be something different from a mixture of opinions about God and the world, and of precepts for one life or for two. Piety cannot be an instinct craving for a mess of metaphysical and ethical crumbs."[39]

Although religion may contain metaphysical and moral conceptions, its essence is to be found not in knowledge or action, but in the nonrational and passive affections of feeling, intuition, taste, sense, and so on. Otto writes that for Schleiermacher

> There is a third relationship to the world: this is not science of the world, neither is it action upon the world; it is *experience* of this world in its profundity, the realization of its eternal content by the feeling of a contemplative and devout mind. This is not science or metaphysics; nor is it ethics or individual effort and directive activity. It is *religion*: the immediate appraisal of the universe as the one and the whole, transcending the mere parts which science may grasp, and at the same time the profound spiritual experience of its underlying ideal essence.[40]

According to Schleiermacher, this third mode of relation to the world consists in the consciousness of the existence of all finite things in and through the infinite, and of all temporal things in and through the eternal: "It is a life in the infinite nature of the whole, in the One and in the All, in God, having and possessing all things in God and God in all. . . . In itself it is an affection and revelation of the Infinite in the finite, God being seen in it and it in God."[41]

Although Otto recognizes that Schleiermacher's account of religion is conditioned by the intellectual situation of the time, certain aspects of Schleiermacher's analysis appear to have a direct influence on Otto's own understanding of religion. First, both Schleiermacher and Otto affirm that religion ultimately depends not on rational factors, but on a nonrational core, and both agree that religion accordingly has its own province in the mind. Second, and in consequence, both agree that all religious discourse, all theological ideas and principles, are or ought to be relatable to affections of the religious consciousness.[42]

Schleiermacher and Otto both argue that any attempt to determine a *rational* universal religion at the core of the world's historical religious traditions is misconceived. Consequently, both find the plurality of religions a necessary and desirable result of religion's universal *nonrational* essence. Opposing the efforts of the Enlightenment to construct a universal religion acceptable to all rational persons, Schleiermacher writes:

> You must abandon the vain and foolish wish that there should be only one religion; you must lay aside all repugnance to its multiplicity; as candidly as possible you must approach everything that has ever, in the changing shapes of humanity, been developed in its advancing career, from the ever fruitful bosom of the spiritual life. . . . The whole of religion is nothing but the sum of all relations of man to God, apprehended in all the possible ways in which any man can be immediately conscious in his life. . . . You are wrong, therefore, with your universal religion that is natural to all, for no one will have his own true and right religion, if it is the same for all.[43]

Otto similarly stresses the unique value of each religion. His argument for the necessity of recognizing the unique value of specific religions is directed not only against rationalism's attempt to formulate a universal religion, but also against what he calls "traditionalism's" attempt to do the same and, in so doing, invariably to assign the role to its own tradition.[44]

For "traditionalism" we might read "Ritschlianism," for there was an incipient tendency in Ritschl's theology as a whole to see religion in exclusively christocentric, bibliocentric, and, one might say, reformationistic terms. Moreover, Ritschl was criticized around the turn of this century by members of the so-called history-of-religions school (Wilhelm Bousset, Wilhelm Heitmüller, Hermann Gunkel, and Ernst Troeltsch) for rejecting Schleiermacher's pluralism in favor of Christian exclusivism. During his time at Göttingen, Otto was prominently associated with both

Troeltsch and Bousset. Be that as it may, Otto writes very much in a Romantic spirit reminiscent of Schleiermacher:

> And we would urge the individual not to be led astray by universalizing analogies and resemblances between religions, but first of all to concentrate upon that which is central and individual in his own religion. We do not mean by this that he should restore the paraphernalia of tradition or the apparatus of an effete dogmatism. . . . We are concerned not to mend old clothes, but to ascertain in its truth and subtlety the individual *spirit* itself of a religion, and thus to set a value upon the particular, the essence of the ideals, sentiments, life and conduct which it produces, to liberate these and give them a new and appropriate form.[45]

Further, it is interesting to note that, although both affirm the desirability of religious pluralism, they nonetheless tend to view Christianity as the end point of the religious process.[46] Neither Schleiermacher nor Otto is able to substantiate this view satisfactorily.

Finally, both Otto and Schleiermacher see religious experience as having a cognitive status. Indeed, Otto is the first in a line of modern commentators upon Schleiermacher who point to the undeniably objective character (for him) of religious consciousness,[47] and thereby stand opposed to that tradition of Schleiermacher interpretation which, from Hegel and Feuerbach to Barth and Brunner, saw Schleiermacher as one enmeshed in inescapable subjectivism. Otto's view of Schleiermacher is quite clear in *Das Heilige*, but it is also present as early as 1899 in Otto's introduction to his edition of the *Speeches on Religion*:

> He [Schleiermacher] wished to show that man is not wholly confined to [scientific] knowledge [*Wissen*] and action, that the relationship of men to their environment—the world, being, mankind, events—is not ex-

hausted in the mere perception or shaping of it. He
sought to prove that if one experienced the environing
world in a state of deep emotion, as intuition and feeling, and that if one were deeply affected by a sense of
its eternal and abiding essence to the point where one
was moved to feelings of devotion, awe, and reverence—then such an affective state was worth more
than knowledge and action put together.[48]

Otto finds his own later commitment to the notion of a
religious a priori in human consciousness outlined in
Schleiermacher's work: "As Kant inquires after and examines the faculty of perception, of the power of judgment, of
understanding, of reason, of theoretical and practical reason
in order to find the essence of knowledge, of moral action,
and of aesthetic taste, so Schleiermacher seeks the faculty
of the mind out of which religion arises."[49]

The Turn to Idealism

All this is not to suggest that Otto's relation to the writings
of Schleiermacher was an uncritical one. Already in the
introduction to his edition of the *Speeches on Religion* he
complains that Schleiermacher neglects the *critical* examination of the autonomous nature of the religious life, a failure in Schleiermacher which was later to be a decisive one
for Otto. Still, in 1899 Otto is very much a disciple of the
first edition of the *Speeches on Religion*. He is critical of the
later revised and edited versions: "the fresh, youthful and
original effusion, which had produced the first direct effects, could no longer be recognized in them."[50] And certainly Schleiermacher gave his later versions fewer rhetorical flourishes and related them much more closely to his
formal dogmatics. Otto also prefers the *Speeches on Religion* to any of Schleiermacher's later works (especially *The
Christian Faith*), since many of these latter "forfeited the

original meaning, richness and impact in the interests of a stricter and more systematic treatment."[51] Five years later, although he was already coming under the influence of the Friesian philosophy, Otto still maintains that Schleiermacher is superior to Fries in his breadth of ideas, even if less incisive in his expressions of them.[52]

By 1909, however, Otto has become a fervent disciple of Fries, and his position vis-à-vis Schleiermacher has changed. In the introduction to *The Philosophy of Religion* he writes:

> Historians of the philosophy of religion have pointed
> to a certain affinity between Fries and Schleiermacher
> in their treatment of the theory of religious "feeling,"
> but they have assumed that Schleiermacher's was the
> more original and comprehensive intellect. Really,
> however, in the philosophy of religion, the points of
> contact between Fries and Schleiermacher are less im-
> portant than their points of difference; and when their
> views agree, Fries is quite original, and closer study
> proves him to be superior in comprehensiveness, thor-
> oughness, and solidity.[53]

This shift from Schleiermacher to Fries entails also a revi-
sion of Otto's views on Kant, for only as a result of Fries's
development of the Kantian philosophy does the philosophy of religion gain a solid philosophical foundation. By
contrast, Schleiermacher offers "primarily a kind of inspired
guesswork . . . and often enough in the *Discourses*
[*Speeches*] the arbitrary decree of genius replaces the solid
reasoning from philosophy and history."[54] In short, in Friesian philosophy Otto was to find the rational foundation for
and the guarantee of his sympathy with Schleiermacher's
position.

Otto's desire for a philosophical framework upon which
to ground the study of religion was also motivated by the
burgeoning of the natural sciences in the late nineteenth
century, and the consequent devaluation of a religious

worldview in the light of the materialistic and naturalistic philosophies which were thus fostered. Schleiermacher's account of religion was of little help in defending religion against this sort of attack. The overall aim of Otto's *Naturalism and Religion* was to defend the religious conception of the world by a vigorous assertion of its autonomous validity, since "the natural sciences, in association with other convictions and aims, tend readily to unite into a distinctive and independent system of world interpretation, which, if it were valid and sufficient, would drive the religious view into difficulties, or make it impossible."[55]

Otto does not want to defend the religious conception of the world by means of a natural theology based on evidences in nature, for he recognizes that such attempts too often ignore the "multitudinous enigmas," the many instances of what seems "unmeaning and purposeless, confused and dark."[56] Nor is he interested in arguing for any form of supernaturalism in which the cause of one part of any event is ascribed to natural causes and that of another part of the same event to the divine, for this conflicts with both the demands of science and the nature of religion. Rather, his aim is to show that what religion demands is compatible with a properly construed philosophy of science:

> It may, for instance, be possible that the mathematical-mechanical interpretation of things, even if it be sufficient within its own domain, does not take away from nature the characters which religion seeks and requires in it, namely, purpose, dependence, and mystery. Or it may be that nature itself does not correspond at all to this ideal of mathematical explicability, that this ideal may well be enough as a guide for investigation, but that it is not a fundamental clue really applying to nature as a whole and in its essence. ... And this suggests another possibility, namely, that the naturalistic method of interpretation cannot be

applied throughout the whole territory of nature . . . and, finally, that it is distinctly interrupted and held in abeyance at particular points by the incommensurable which breaks forth spontaneously out of the depths of phenomena revealing a depth which is not to be explained away.[57]

Dependence, mystery, purpose—these are the three elements of human experience and existence with which, according to Otto, religion uniquely concerns itself, and which cannot be accounted for in a naturalistic conception of the world. One passage may suffice to indicate the direction of Otto's argument. He writes that in religion we find

first, the interest, never to be relinquished, of experiencing and acknowledging the world and existence to be a mystery, and regarding all that is known and manifested in things merely as the thin crust which separates us from the uncomprehended and inexpressible. Secondly, there is the desire on the part of religion to bring ourselves and all creatures into the "feeling of absolute dependence". . . . Finally, there is the interest in a theological interpretation of the world as opposed to the purely causal interpretation of natural science.[58]

Just as Otto saw German idealism as a bulwark against the French materialism of the eighteenth century, so also he views Kantian idealism as the means whereby autonomy may be accorded to both religion and science in the nineteenth and twentieth centuries. While science deals with the phenomenal realm, the distinction between it and the noumenal allows for the possible reality of those "objects" to which religion avers. This is not to suggest that Otto adopts Kantianism outright, for he is quite aware, on the one hand, that Kant had placed religion outside the realm of knowledge, and, on the other, that even if religion had remained within the bounds of knowledge as defined by Kant, this would not satisfy the demands of religion: "Now for a student of natural science it may perhaps be of no importance whether the category he applies in his investigation . . . is only a form of the world of his ideas, or whether the world of reality corresponds to it and is obedient to it: for the religious man it is not a matter of indifference. Nay, rather for him everything is absolutely dependent on the valency of religious ideas apart from his own conception of them."[59]

Otto turned to Fries in order to resolve the problem of the validity of religion inherent within the Kantian scheme. Why to the philosophy of Fries rather than, say, to the neo-Kantianism of Hermann Lotze which had been (loosely) woven by Ritschl into his theology? Partly because of the efforts of the neo-Friesians to recruit Otto to their cause. And despite Otto's suggestion to the contrary, it can also be partly attributed to the similarities between Fries and Schleiermacher in their mutual emphasis on "feeling" as the basis of religion. (To be sure, Fries was more influenced by Kant's third critique, the *Critique of Judgment*, than by Romanticism.[60])

Troeltsch's negative judgment upon Ritschl's alliance with the neo-Kantianism of Lotze may also have been indirectly significant in Otto's becoming a Friesian. Certainly, anti-Ritschlianism was being aired in Göttingen, and from the beginning of his academic career Troeltsch had consistently rejected Ritschl's use of Kant's distinction between faith and knowledge to ground religion in value judgments.[61] For example, Troeltsch writes, "By placing all the emphasis upon the separation of theoretical and practical reason and stressing only the practical necessity of the values claimed by religion, they [the value-judgment theorists] lose the necessity of the object to which these values are attached and plunge into the abyss of a theology based on human desires and illusions."[62] Troeltsch himself may be criticized here for undervaluing the cognitive import of the notion of value judgments, and for thereby providing grist for the anti-Ritschlian mill. Still, the point remains that the philosophical foundations of Ritschlianism were seen as unviable. Moreover, Otto may have been more positively influenced by Troeltsch by virtue of the latter's own commitment to a form of neo-Kantianism without which, Troeltsch remarks, "one is tied down in advance to the impossibility of an epistemological or cognitive value in religion."[63]

I do not intend to suggest that Otto was able to or even wanted to cast off all vestiges of Ritschl's thought. Ritschlianism was dominant and very pervasive, and elements of it do appear in *Das Heilige*. Nevertheless, its insufficiency in providing Otto with an adequate philosophical grounding for religion probably played a role in his adoption of the philosophy of Fries.

Otto and Fries

We have seen that, for Kant, experience is the product of the given of experience (which has for us a spatio-temporal form) and the a priori categories of the understanding. For Kant, the a priori nature of the forms of intuition and the categories is sufficient to disprove their objective validity. Jakob Fries (1773–1843), although an avowed disciple of Kant's philosophy, disagrees on this point. He maintains that knowledge of reality in itself is possible—in the negative knowledge of rational faith, and in the positive knowledge afforded by intuitive feeling. In Fries's view, human understanding may be divided in a threefold way: scientific knowledge (*Wissen*), rational faith (*Glaube*), and religio-aesthetic intuition (*Ahndung*)—independent but interrelated forms of knowledge, with the latter two being higher forms.[64]

The foundation for Fries's argument is laid in his discussion of the nature of truth.[65] In an idealist system such as Kant's, truth cannot be defined as the agreement of an idea with its object, for, on the one hand, there is no means by which we can compare the object as known with the object independent of knowledge. (Apart from perception and cognition themselves, there are no checking procedures.[66]) We must have *immediate* knowledge that there is a world independent of our perceptions. On the other hand, truth as customarily defined cannot explain our knowledge of necessary truths, that is, truths independent of experience. To account for our knowledge of their validity, we must have *immediate* knowledge of them also. Truth expressed in rational judgments finally depends, therefore, upon "the agreement of the judgment with the immediate knowledge of reason on which it is based."[67] Although this immediate knowledge of reason can only be laid bare by the empirical examination of our mental processes, that is, in an *anthropologische Kritik* (anthropological critique), it possesses its own criterion of truth, a *Wahrheitsgefühl* (feeling of truth) which is inescapable and irreducible. Otto explains,

> The fact that we really *know* something in our sense perceptions, i.e., that we conceive an object which really exists and conceive it according to its being, is solely based on Reason's natural self-confidence that it is capable of truth and knowledge. . . . This applies with no less force—rather with more—to a priori kinds of real knowledge than to such as depend on sense perception. Those "self-evident" truths, which every child grasps at once, are valid for Reason, as laws for the objective world itself. . . . the condition in which immediate knowledge shows itself as active, even before light has penetrated to its primal obscurity is the *Feeling of Truth*.[68]

As Otto indicates in this passage, the content of this immediate knowledge of Reason is that of the objective reality of Being and existence in general. Furthermore, in this immediate knowledge is revealed the unity and necessity of that which is given to sense perception: "Each and everything in general is a *synthetic unity*, i.e., constitutes a whole, in the complete connection of its elements, a coherent world of Being and Happening. Not a hotch-potch of disparate and disconnected phenomena, of which there could be no experience, no observation, no science, which would be blind and senseless, a mere 'rhapsody of perceptions'; not this but an association of thorough and coherent interdependence."[69] Moreover, not a synthetic unity which has occurred by chance, but one which is necessarily so.

According to Fries, the a priori categories of understanding articulate the only possible forms of this immediate knowledge of reason—the idea of universal unity and necessity. Therefore the categories give us knowledge of objective reality, of the noumenal realm. According to Kant, we can have no real knowledge by means of the *pure* a priori categories, but only by means of these when schematized by the a priori forms of intuition. In contrast to this, according to Fries, the categories lose their absolute validity and are limited and restricted as a result of this schematizing. Our knowledge of the world through the schematized categories is incomplete and imperfect, in comparison to the purely rational interpretation of reality embedded in our immediate knowledge of Reason and expressed in the *pure* categories of the understanding.

Fries argues that, in the Ideas of Reason—God, the soul, and freedom—which for Kant are at most regulative ideals in the pursuit of scientific knowledge, we have a completely rational knowledge of reality, and that the realm of scientific knowledge (*Wissen*) allows transitions to this pure rational knowledge (*Glaube*). By applying to the incomplete and imperfect temporally schematized categories, especially those under the head of *relation*, an ideal schematism by which the categories are *completed*, the *Ideas* of Reason are able to be deduced directly. As R. F. Davidson comments, "the restriction and limitation imposed by the data of sense-experience upon the conceptual knowledge of the phenomenal world is removed and an ideal view of reality as a completely intelligible world of rational being is achieved."[70]

More specifically, the Ideas of the soul, freedom, and God are derived from the ideal schematism of the categories of subsistence and inherence (substance and accident), causality and dependence (cause and effect), and community (interaction between agent and patient), respectively. The removal of temporal schematism from the first of the above categories entails the disappearance of the quantitative aspects of material objects (extension, motion, change of motion and position) but the retention of their qualitative attributes—both outer qualities (color, sound, odor, warmth, hardness, etc.) and their inner correlates (pleasure, feeling, volition, desire, anger, hate, etc.). Otto writes, "In the individual (personal) mind with its 'inner qualities' do we alone know with certitude and clearness what substances are. By way of analogy to it we interpret that which is, then, as a world of spiritual being and life, of spiritual substances in general."[71] This, according to Otto, is the meaning contained in the notion of soul. So also with the category of cause and effect: when ideal schematism is applied, causation is no longer restricted to temporal succession, and there is the possibility of a cause which is not the result of another cause: "the category of causality becomes the Idea of the Free Will of spiritual Substances."[72] Finally, the category of community (that objects constitute a system the parts of which mutually exclude and mutually determine each other), when ideally schematized, points to "the operation of one unified, essential, necessary, extramundane cause of all in general"[73] which orders things in accord with final purpose, that is, God.

By negating or completing the temporally schematized categories (which are themselves negations or limitations of the pure categories), we gain that knowledge which is articulated in the pure categories, namely, knowledge of the "thing-in-itself." Although for Fries this purely rational knowledge is higher than that gained by means of the operation of the schematized categories, since the Ideas of Reason arise by *negation*, we have *no positive* knowledge of them. We know *that* they are, but not *what* they are. All we can do is deny that the limitations of empirical existence apply to them.[74]

Kant found that God, freedom, and immortality arose as necessary postulates of the demands of practical reason. According to Fries, however, religious faith is not an outcome of the demands of the moral law. Rather, moral consciousness is itself conditioned by the immediate knowledge of reason, and therefore by the Ideas of Reason. The categorical imperative is itself determined by the existence of an absolute objective value which is reflected in all finite valuing. Otto writes:

> All the values of our existence as appearing in Time can be high, very high; they can never be absolutely high. To all finite value we oppose the absolutely completed value in the word "Dignity" [*Würde*]. It is applicable to that which, under the Idea, was conceived absolutely as Substance: the spirit of the person in its independence and freedom from the machinery of Nature as a whole. "Dignity of the Person" is the ideal principle under which we judge every man, as the appearance of an eternal and personal spirit.[75]

Moreover—and this becomes especially important for Otto's work on ethics toward the end of his life—in the dignity of the person is manifested an eternal worth and purpose, not only of the individual, but of the world as a whole:

> Ethics has given us the values and the purposes, which are possible for men as individuals, for humanity as a whole in the course of its history. . . . In the forms of ideal knowledge, however . . . it becomes the faith in the absolute value of Being in itself, in the *objective purpose* and the objective purposiveness of the

real universe itself, which, on account of its holy and all powerful cause, the Godhead, dwells in man and by means of this becomes for him the "Highest Good."[76]

For Fries, religion is to be aware of this eternal purpose, and to live in accord with it.

Like God, the soul, and freedom, the objective purposiveness of the universe remains as negative knowledge in the realm of *Glaube*. What, then, of the relationship between that which is negatively known in *Glaube* about objective reality and that which is known through *Wissen* of the same objective reality that merely appears to us through the manifold senses? For Fries, the connection is provided through feeling: "knowledge of the Eternal in the finite is only possible through pure feeling."[77] Through *Ahndung*, which (like logical judgments) is characterized by an immediate feeling of truth, it is revealed that the world of scientific knowledge is really ordered in agreement with the principles of rational faith.[78] Otto remarks:

> Feeling, with Knowledge and Faith, gives a third kind of real knowledge, one which combines and unifies both of these—"Ahnen." Obscure sentiments of the beautiful and sublime in all its phases, in the natural and spiritual life, have us in their power: and so we understand without any medium the Eternal in the Temporal, and the Temporal as an appearance of the Eternal. Intelligibly enough, positively, although beyond our powers of expression, the world of Faith here manifests itself in the world of Knowledge by means of "Ahnung."[79]

Neither *Glaube* nor *Ahndung* can be positively expressed, but the latter can be positively felt. As we shall see later, neither the rational nor the nonrational sides of the divine can be spoken of positively, though the nonrational is positively felt.

It is through *Ahndung* that religion arises,[80] for piety may be identified (according to Fries) with the enthusiasm, devotion, and self-surrender to God which result from it, and the consciousness of eternal destiny, of good and evil, of sin and responsibility that are inescapably connected with it. And, most important for Otto's later account of religious knowledge, all statements which derive from it are mere approximations, since *Ahndung* "is utterly incapable of being analyzed and is absolutely proof against presentation in conceptual form."[81]

We shall later see the extent of Otto's dependence on Fries in his mature philosophy of religion. For the moment, suffice it to say that in Fries's idealism Otto finds a rational framework for his conviction that religion is in its essence nonrational. The experience of its nonrational essence is formally identical with the experience of *Ahndung*, and the connection between *Glaube* and *Ahndung* later provides Otto with a model of the connection between the rational and nonrational elements of religion, and of our objective knowledge of these. All of these depend, in the final analysis, on the fact that in Friesianism Otto found a philosophical scheme which guaranteed the autonomy of religion and provided a defense against the onslaught of materialistic and naturalistic reductions of it.

There was one point at which Otto went beyond the Friesian position, even at the time of *The Philosophy of Religion*. Otto sees the possibility of *Ahndung* including the realization of the operation of the eternal in history. While Schleiermacher was his primary influence here, the Friesian theologian Wilhelm de Wette (1780–1849) was undoubtedly also important, for it was he who specifically attempted to apply the Friesian concept of *Ahndung* to the historical realm, a use to which Otto was to put the concept in *Das Heilige*.[82]

In the conclusion to *The Philosophy of Religion* Otto foreshadows his future work. He maintains that the science of religion will have "two separate starting points and will follow two paths, at first different, which, however, lead to each other and must meet at last."[83] The first of these is an empirical examination of religion which will "secure by induction an empirical conception of the properties, character, and real nature of Religion as a whole."[84] The starting point for this will be religious experience. The other path will follow the work of the *Critique of Reason* as a whole which finds its completion, and the means for the interpretation of religious experience, in *Ahndung*.

The former path finds its culmination in *Das Heilige*; the latter is already well developed in *The Philosophy of Religion*. Surprisingly, in Otto's subsequent works there are few clear indications of the conjunction of these two paths. Indeed, references to Friesian philosophy are few and far between. For the moment, it is sufficient to note that Otto's psychological analysis of the contents of the religious consciousness is not compatible with the content of *Ahndung*; his commitment to the specifics of Friesianism becomes less forthright as a result. This is not to imply that Friesianism is of no importance in Otto's later philosophical theology; on the contrary, it continues to provide the philosophical substructure, in method if not in content. But it is not overtly present, and therefore it needs to be discerned beneath the surface of Otto's method and language. As we shall see in the next two chapters, it can be teased out of his account of the "empirical" path and out of the later philosophical stance he develops to interpret his empirical findings.

3
The Numinous Experience

The Holy

According to Otto, religions consist of both rational and nonrational elements. And, as the subtitle of *Das Heilige* makes clear, Otto's purpose in that volume is to investigate the nonrational factor in religion and its relation to the rational. In this chapter and the next we shall examine Otto's account of these elements and the philosophical presuppositions on which it is based. We shall thereby explore as far as possible the continuity and discontinuity between the ideas, both latent and manifest, in *Das Heilige* and in Otto's earlier work.

Our initial task is to try to clarify what Otto means by "rational" and "nonrational." Generally, we identify the rational with thinking and the nonrational with feeling. For Otto, however, the application of the terms "rational" and "nonrational" is determined not so much by reference to thinking and feeling as by reference *to the objects* of thinking and feeling. That is to say, "rational" and "nonrational" are primarily predicates of objects, and only secondarily a thinking or a feeling about objects. Whether or not an object is in any particular instance thought or felt, it is nonetheless a rational object to the extent that it can be thought conceptually.[1] In contrast, whether or not an object is felt or thought, it is a nonrational object insofar as it cannot be brought "into the domain of the conceptual understanding."[2] In short, in Kantian terms, a rational object is one which can be thought under the a priori categories of understanding; a nonrational object is one which cannot be so thought.

The referent of religion, that is, the Holy, is for Otto both a rational and a nonrational object. To be sure, there is a lack of clarity in Otto's argument at this point, but we can nonetheless discern its major thrust. On the one hand, the Holy (or God) can be thought of as a rational object, because he is possessed of a rational nature. That is to say, where deity is characterized by the attributes spirit, reason, purpose, good will, supreme power, unity, and selfhood, it can in some sense be brought into the sphere of understanding since it is "thus thought of by analogy with our human nature of reason and personality."[3]

But there is an important difference between these attributes when applied to human nature on the one hand and the divine nature on the other. That such attributes are only to be predicated of the nature of deity *analogously* is because they are thought of as "completed" when applied to God, in contrast to our awareness of them as "qualified by restriction and limitation" in ourselves.[4] Otto is clearly drawing, if only loosely, on the Friesian deduction of the Ideas of Reason by the negation of the limitations imposed upon them by temporal schematism. His argument may be constructed as follows. Both God and human beings are rational objects, and the attributes of human nature are applicable to deity. Since human beings can be conceived of as having spirit, reason, purpose, etc., they are rational objects and are thought under the limitations imposed by temporal schematism. Because God is not an object that can be thought under such limitations, such attributes may be thought of as applicable to God only where the limitations imposed by reason are removed.

On the other hand, the Holy is also—and preeminently—a nonrational object. Indeed, Otto wants to suggest that the rational attributes, far from exhausting the idea of deity, "in fact are only directly about and of validity for a *Nonratio-*

nal,"[5] which is inaccessible to conceptual thought and can only be felt.

Feeling can refer to both rational and nonrational objects.[6] Insofar as feeling is referrable to an object which can be identified in precise conceptual terms, it comes within the domain of the rational. But when feeling is evoked by a nonrational object—that is, the nonrational side of the divine—it is qualitatively unique. While there are analogies between nonrational and rational feelings, the uniqueness and irreducibility of the former is due to its being evoked by a nonrational object.[7] Otto's argument for the sui generis nature of nonrational (that is, religious) feelings is grounded largely in their being intimately related to the apprehension of a sui generis nonrational object, and his psychological comparison of the religious consciousness and the rational consciousness, which intends to demonstrate the qualitative uniqueness of the contents of the former, presupposes this.

Empirical religions, then, are complexes of unique (because *completed*) rational elements and unique nonrational elements. Such complexes arise, according to Otto, from a "category of interpretation and valuation peculiar to the sphere of religion"[8] which he calls the category of the Holy (*die Kategorie des Heiligen*). Religion arises as the result of the attribution of holiness to something by means of the operation of this category of the mind. This means that holiness is not merely another phenomenon of religion, like belief in gods and demons, meditation, creation myths, sacrifice, and so on.[9] Rather, all these and other various phenomena which are putatively religious can be reckoned as such in terms of it.

The rational elements of the Holy bear an analogous relation to elements of human nature. The nonrational elements likewise are analogous to rational feelings, but they are nonetheless unique and constitute the core of religion. Otto writes, "There is no religion in which it does not live as the real innermost core and without it no religion would be worthy of the name."[10] To this core of religion Otto applies the term *numinous* (*numinös*) which he derives from the Latin word for divinity, *numen*.[11] He later writes that, in contrast to any reduction of religion into nonreligious terms, his position is

> that "religion begins of itself." That does not mean that religion was there right from the beginning. It means even less that it began with an elementary theism. Rather, it means that we have to reckon at the beginning of religious developments themselves with an element that . . . on all levels of religion and also in its most competing expressions is discoverable as an immediate fundamental element. It is present in the richest faith in God as in the so different mystical experience of unity, and of the One in which all diversity of mundane being is immersed; and it is active already in elementary and "crude" form in the completely unique primitive feeling of the "wholly other" at early stages. We call this element "the numinous feeling."[12]

A numinous state of mind is one which occurs when the category of the Holy is applied. Consequently, the attribution of holiness is ineluctably connected to the numinous experiences.

Sources of the Holy

The notion that the attribution of holiness is of central importance to religion is not unique to Otto, although he certainly gave it an original flavor. The term *holiness* and its cognate *holy* had restricted currency in German thought prior to the twentieth century. In German philosophical literature, *Heiligkeit* or a cognate thereof appeared in the writings of Kant, Schleiermacher, Hegel, and Nietzsche, but by no means in Otto's sense. *Heilig* played a small role in the poetry of, for example, Hölderlin and Goethe,[13] and it is used, but again not in Otto's sense, by both Fries and De Wette.[14]

The terms gained intellectual currency early in the twentieth century through Wilhelm Windelband (1848–1915), the leader of the Southwestern German or Baden school of neo-Kantianism. It has been suggested in a number of places that Otto was familiar with and influenced (although perhaps only negatively) by Windelband.[15] That Otto was familiar with the work of Windelband is quite likely, although no reference to Windelband appears in any of Otto's writings. Perhaps any influence was mediated via Ernst Troeltsch. Troeltsch criticized Windelband for threatening the autonomy of religion, a criticism with which Otto would have fully concurred.

In 1902, an essay entitled "Das Heilige" was added to Windelband's two-volume *Präludien: Aufsätze und Reden zur Einführung in die Philosophie*, first published in 1884.[16] According to this, the entire province of the activity of the mind is subsumable under the three rational activities of thought, will, and feeling; out of these arise three kinds of rational values (the logical, the ethical, and the aesthetic) that are alone the data of philosophical inquiry. For Windelband, religious valuations do not arise from an autonomous rational mode of valuing or from any nonrational activity or impulse of the mind. Rather, religion is the relating of logical, ethical, and aesthetic values to a transphenomenal realm, "to a supramundane, superempirical, suprasensuous reality."[17] The holy is not merely the *relation* of these values to a higher reality, but it is also the ground of them. The notion of value demands an absolute value, "a metaphysical anchorage,"[18] from which all mundane valuing ultimately derives its validity.

In spite of the fact that both Otto and Windelband are united against any reductionist accounts of religion, Windelband's rational derivation of religion and his stress on the nonautonomous nature of religion would not have been attractive to Otto during his neo-Friesian period. Like Troeltsch, he would have seen Windelband's thesis as the thin end of a wedge cutting toward the collapse of religious autonomy. For the neo-Friesian Otto, religion is essentially nonrational and immediately given in the experience of *Ahndung*. Windelband's thesis would not be appropriate for the Otto of *Das Heilige*, because according to this work religion arises from its own unique nonrational source.

Still, if we must trace to Windelband the philosophical origins of the twentieth-century use of the term *heilig*, for its use as a term in the interpretation of the history of religions we must turn to the Swedish theologian Nathan Söderblom (1866–1931). Though it has been argued that, for his uses of the term, Otto is directly dependent on Söderblom, there is no direct evidence to suggest such a dependence. Indeed, such evidence as there is suggests that they were simultaneously and independently working on parallel lines.

In 1913, Söderblom's essay on "Holiness" appeared in the sixth volume of Hasting's *Encyclopaedia of Religion and Ethics*. The ideas contained therein were developed in his important book *Gudstrons uppkommst*, published in 1914 and translated into German in 1916 under the title *Das Werden des Gottesglaubens* (*The Origin of Belief in God*).[19] For Söderblom, as for Otto, the attribution of holiness is the essence of religion: "Holiness is the great word in religion; it is even more essential than the notion of God. Real religion may exist without a definite conception of divinity, but there is no real religion without a distinction between holy and profane."[20]

Meanwhile, already in January, 1913, we can see developing the sense which Otto was to bring to the term *heilig*:

> You know Isaiah 6, where the Seraphim standing
> around sing: holy, holy, holy is the Lord Sabaoth.
> What do they mean by it, and what do we mean,
> when we repeat this hymn of the angels? Do we mean

that Yahweh is the principle of higher moral perfection? It is very often meant in this way: holy. But
"holy" does not signify that. "Holy" denotes a unique
term that is not definable, that is not explainable
through other terms, but must be experienced; para-
phrasing generally, we can perhaps say: that mysterious transcendent in general that lives in the religious
feeling of devotion and humility.[21]

Moreover, although Söderblom, like Otto, sees "holiness"
as meaning more than the purely ethical, it is Otto who, by
his concept of the category of the Holy, attempts to account
in a much more systematic fashion for the relation between
the moral and nonmoral, or supramoral, aspects of holiness.[22]

Through the notion of holiness, Söderblom attempts to
trace a continuity between more primitive forms of religious life and the most highly developed religions, this both
subjectively and objectively. Subjectively, the origin of the
conceptions of holiness "seems to have been the mental
reaction against what is startling, astonishing, new, terri-
fying."[23] Objectively, holiness is a power—*mana, orenda,
wakanda*, etc.—connected with certain objects, beings, and
events, the reaction to which is *religious* experience. In
short, through the concept of holiness Söderblom attempts
to find a principle of connection in the continually burgeoning knowledge of empirical religions during the late nineteenth and early twentieth centuries. Otto must be seen as
attempting to do the same, but he does not seem to have
derived the notion of holiness as a power inherent in things,
persons, and so on, from Söderblom. Rather, as we shall see
when we examine his analysis of Wundt's *Völkerpsychologie*, Otto had come to much the same conclusion independently,[24] and certainly by the time of *Das Heilige* he had
progressed significantly beyond Söderblom in his more
finely tuned analysis of the religious consciousness.

Indeed, in early 1915, in a review of Söderblom's *Guds-*

trons uppkommst, Otto clearly gives the impression that he and Söderblom are working on parallel lines with regard to their views on the origin of religion. He goes as far as to criticize Söderblom's claim that Yahweh, the God of the Old Testament, has his point of origin in animism. On the contrary, Otto argues, such beings as Yahweh are born not from a belief in spirits, but from a religious awe peculiar to the sphere of religion.[25] Here, too, is foreshadowed Otto's subsequent criticism of Söderblom to the effect that the latter fails to stress sufficiently the qualitative difference between religious and other natural feelings. Otto levels the same criticism at the English anthropologist R. R. Marett, while admitting that Marett nonetheless "comes within a hair's breadth of what I take to be the truth about the matter."[26] In his later version in 1932 of his article on Wundt, Otto sharpens his criticism of Söderblom and Marett still further: "I repeat my objection that the 'manist' too does not solve the chief problem, for by the term 'power' neither Mana nor Orenda is explained. It is a power pertaining to a 'wholly other' sphere which I tried to circumscribe by symbols of the numinous. It is power 'numinously apperceived,' and it is this original faculty of numinous apperception which is the thing that matters."[27]

In sum, while Otto and Söderblom both use the term *holiness* as a key to the interpretation of religious phenomena, Otto fills the term with a content which both parallels and surpasses Söderblom's, not least in his unique combining of "holiness" as a philosophical concept (a usage which he may well owe to Windelband) with "holiness" as a key interpretative concept in the psychological analysis of the religious consciousness.

This psychological approach to religion may date from the late eighteenth century, making its appearance in the analyses of religion of such varied thinkers as Herder, Jacobi, Schleiermacher, and Fries, and in the religious critiques of Feuerbach, Marx, and Nietzsche. Twentieth-century German work in the psychological analysis of religion was given its decisive impetus by the growth in North America of experimental psychology and the psychology of religion developed by, for instance, J. H. Leuba, E. D. Starbuck, and, most important, William James.

The importance of this development for Otto lies not only in the fact that such books as James's *Varieties of Religious Experience* provided a wealth of source material, but also in the fact that they showed that analysis of the religious consciousness need not proceed from any a priori theory. Instead, it could proceed from the consideration of how *empirically* it is actually constituted. Yet, it is exactly in the attempt to interweave his empirico-psychological account of religion with his theoretical assumptions as to how it ought to be that the fabric of Otto's analysis unravels. The empirical analysis of religious states of consciousness does imply a *variety* of religious experiences, whereas, by contrast, the presuppositions of Otto's philosophical analysis of the Holy entail a *unity* of religious experience.

Be that as it may, one of the most significant outcomes of the developing German interest in empirical psychology is the work of Wilhelm Wundt (1832–1920), in particular, for our purposes, his magisterial ten-volume study *Völkerpsychologie* (1900–1920). Wundt is often rightly thought of as the father of empirical psychology, yet he was also willing to accept certain kinds of data not amenable to precise measurement—namely, those which inhere not in the individual but in the social community. The study of the psychology of the community, of its origins and developments, is essential to psychology, maintains Wundt, if it is to qualify as a science. Otto is especially concerned with the two volumes of the *Völkerpsychologie* that deal with the origins and development of myth and religion from the psychology of society as a whole.

According to Wundt, religion is rationally derived from the concept of souls. It evolves through the stage of ghosts and demons until the idea of gods and the absolute Godhead is reached. Wundt's account parallels in form, if not in specific details, a number of other contemporaneous accounts of the "rational" origin of religion. It is important here because Wundt's analysis first arouses Otto's interest in the so-called primitive religions, because it provides a crucial link in the chain connecting the Friesian Otto with the Otto of *Das Heilige*, and not least because it arouses Otto to defend the autonomy of religion in the context of the most recent attempts to explain it in nonreligious terms.

For example, in a clear statement of the direction in which his thought is heading, Otto writes of the object of religious experience:

> "Numen" would be a happier word for it, simply because one cannot say what that is. And the roots of the numina do *not* lie in soul conceptions. The numen that loiters in the secret dread of hollows or caves, found amongst men all over the world as stimulating and calling forth the sense of "awe," the numen of the deserts and of regions of terror, of the mountain and the ravine, of haunted places and of overpowering natural phenomena, can only by a great stretch of imagination be referred to an idea of "soul," or to any other clear conception.[28]

Not only does the *tremendum* element of the numinous experience thereby reach its first expression, but also, in this same essay, the numinous is seen as "fascination" and as *mysterium*: "At the same time and from the beginning, this awe has a strange interest about itself, a peculiar fascination that nonetheless draws one to the dreadful and unspeakably frightful, captivated with a sense of bewildered craving."[29] And, "From the beginning onward, religion is experience of the Mysterium and a drawing toward and impulse toward the Mysterium—an experience which breaks forth from the depths of the life of feeling as the feeling of the transcendent and as the result of external stimulations and occasions."[30] In a later version of this article the ideas of the earlier are much more developed in terms derived from *Das Heilige*, and they are reinforced by material drawn from his later work in the history of religions. Nevertheless, the framework of Otto's later account of the numinous experience is already established in 1910.

This essay looks not only forward to *Das Heilige*, but also backward to Otto's earlier philosophical work. Already Otto wants to argue that the clarification of the processes of development of the history of religions is to be gained not, as Wundt had claimed, by examining the transition of one form of religion into another, but by the connection of the manifold empirical phenomena of religion to the "creative powers of the rational spirit itself,"[31] that is, in the connection of what is given to a something that is already there.[32] This both bears the impress of Kant and Fries and looks forward to its full explication in the category of the Holy.

Talking about the Numinous

As is well known, Otto uses the terms *mysterium tremendum fascinans et augustum* to describe the *numen* as manifested in the numinous experience. Before going on to examine each of these terms in some detail, it is important to be clear (at least as clear as Otto allows us to be) on how he sees the nature and function of religious language. Earlier in this chapter I made the point that the attributes of the rational side of the Holy are only applicable where the limitations imposed by reason are removed. This holds true also for talk about the nonrational side of the divine. All discussion of the nonrational core of religion falls short of its nonrational referent. It can be spoken of only through the use of ideograms that symbolically and evocatively indicate it:

> More of the experience lives in reverent attitude and gesture, in tone and voice and demeanor, expressing

its momentousness, and in the solemn devotional assembly of a congregation at prayer, than in all the
phases and negative nomenclature which we have
found to designate it. Indeed, these never give a positive suggestion of the object to which the religious
consciousness refers; they are only of assistance
insofar as they profess to indicate *an* object, which
they at the same time contrast with another, at once
distinct from and inferior to it, e.g., "the invisible,"
"the eternal" (non-temporal), "the supernatural," "the
transcendent." Or they are simply ideograms for the
unique content of feeling, ideograms to understand
which a man must already have had the experience
himself.[33]

In short, like the Ideas of Reason and *Ahndung*, the rational
and nonrational sides of the Holy can only be spoken of
negatively. But, also like *Ahndung*, the nonrational side of
the Holy can be positively felt, and only in such positive
feeling of the *numen* can the individual become aware that
such language has actual application. For instance, of the
ideogram *mysterium* Otto writes: "The term does not de-
fine the object more positively in its qualitative character.
But though what is enunciated in the word is negative,
what is meant is something absolutely and intensely positive. This pure positive we can experience in feelings, feelings which our discussion can help to make clear to us,
insofar as it arouses them actually in our hearts."[34]

Here, then, Otto suggests that in order to understand religion we must believe, and belief is very much dependent
on being a recipient of the experience of the *numen*. This
view parallels some more recent developments in the philosophy of religion typified in the writings of, for example,
Norman Malcolm, D. Z. Phillips, Peter Winch, and W. D.
Hudson; in addition, it reminds one of the explanation of
Otto's somewhat discouraging (if only rhetorical) statement
at the beginning of *Das Heilige*, that readers who have not

had a moment of deeply felt religious experience should read no further.[35]

Here also is the reason why theology must remain a rather tentative activity, for while the Holy can be thought, it cannot, so to speak, be thought out. The positive experience and its corresponding negative language do bear some analogy to each other; yet it is impossible to determine the exact nature of this relationship, or how far the analogy extends, because any account of the divine nature, whether of its rational or nonrational side, is fundamentally a way of indicating that the properties of the divine are analogous to yet radically unlike their earthly analogs. We have in Otto, therefore, as in much traditional Western rational theology, a complex accounting of divine attributes with a large amount of uncertainty about what these attributes mean when applied.

What is clear is that, according to Otto, theology has erred where it has positively construed any religious concept or doctrine. Hence, for example, he writes of the doctrine of predestination, "It is an attempted statement, in conceptual terms and by *analogy*, of something that at bottom is incapable of explication by concepts. Fully justified in this sense as an analogical expression, it is wholly unjustified (*summum jus* becoming *summa injuria*) if its character as analogy is missed, so that it is taken as an adequate formulation of theological theory."[36] We need to keep in mind this view of the nature of religious language as we examine *mysterium tremendum fascinans et augustum*.

Mysterium

The numinous experience has both subjective and objective aspects. On the subjective side, it is an awareness of the nothingness of the self over against that by which it is confronted in the numinous experience. This nothingness is both ontological and valuational. On the one hand, the individual's own being is as nothing in the face of the overwhelming might of the other; on the other, alongside this creature-consciousness or creature-feeling, the individual's own *value*, indeed the value of existence in general, is as nothing in the light of the unsurpassable value of the *numen*. Concomitant with these feelings of ontological and valuational nothingness, the *numen* is objectively and immediately apprehended as *mysterium*.

The mental reaction which arises as a result of numinous *mysterium* is stupor, "an astonishment that strikes us dumb, amazement absolute."[37] Consequently, the mysterious is the "wholly other," "that which is quite beyond the sphere of the usual, the intelligible, and the familiar, which therefore falls quite outside the limits of the 'canny,' and is contrasted with it, filling the mind with blank wonder and astonishment."[38] Otto may have adopted the phrase *the wholly other* (*das ganz Andere*) from Jakob Fries,[39] but even so, he filled the term with a content much richer than did Fries, using it against any attempt to confine religion within the web of human reason. As Bernhard Häring points out, "The expression *das ganz Andere* . . . has been chosen by Otto, in order to make it clear against Windelband and others that religion is not simply the holding together of other (intra-mundane) notions of value, that God in contrast to all earthly categories is something wholly other."[40]

Moreover, the substance of the expression was generated by Otto's own analyses of the history of religions. For example, in the *numen* experienced as *mysterium* lies the source of all that in Christian theology is called the *via negativa*. Of John Chrysostom's notion of God as ἀκατάληπτον (incomprehensible) Otto remarks:

> The ἀκατάληπτον involves a denial of conceptual designations, and hence come the negative attributes of deity, which Chrysostom frequently employs, singly or in series—a *negativa theologia* in little. But this

"negative theology" does not mean that faith and feeling are dissipated and reduced to nothing; on the contrary, it contains within it the loftiest spirit of devotion, and it is out of such "negative" attributes that Chrysostom fashions the most solemn confessions and prayers.[41]

Likewise, Otto traces the origins of the doctrine of the simplicity of God (*simplicitas Dei*) to the *numen* as "wholly other." He also finds the scholastic doctrine that God's essence and attributes are identical and that his accidents are interchangeably identical to be an expression of this aspect of the *numen*. This concept is reflected also in the classic Indian texts, the Upanishads: "The spontaneous recognition of this *simplicitas* is actually implicit in the Upanishad saying, negative though it be, 'it [Brahman] is not thus, it is not thus.' For that saying excludes not only predicates, but also the manifoldness of predicability, and therefore implies absolute simplicity."[42]

The notion of the Holy as "the wholly other" also entails a number of important ideas as to the relationship between God and the world. First, it implies that God is not determined by the forms of time and space, that is, not such as can be apprehended under the a priori forms of intuition. Second, whereas simple theism sees God as determined by number, the notion of "wholly other" entails the rejection of any such determination. Therefore, remarks Otto, the word *monotheism* has no positive value but only the negative value of excluding polytheism. Third, this notion entails discarding the idea that God is determinable by the category of cause in relation to the world as effect: "The divine transcends not only time and place, not only measure and number, but all categories of the reason as well. It leaves subsisting only that transcendent basic relationship which is not amenable to any category."[43] What is important here is that the analysis of the religious consciousness, or that part of it which apprehends the *numen* as *myste-*

rium, is conducted in Kantian terms, and with the implication that a proper analysis of the religious consciousness entails the Kantian limits on the scope of religion. But whereas for Kant these limits meant the unknowability in principle of the object of religion, for Otto they place limits on our ability to think about the *numen,* but not on our capacity to know the divine experientially. Thus, for instance, Otto sees the doctrine that God is the *esse* or being of all things as an unjustified attempt to speak *positively* about the relationship of God to the world, to bring the divine, as it were, within the categories of human reason. On the contrary, Otto maintains, it is in effect a negative *formula* of the fundamental relation between God and the world that cannot be conceptually contained: "the formula that God is the being itself of things, or is being in general, endeavors somehow to realize the quite incomprehensible transcendent relationship of God to the world, and to dissociate it from all rational forms of relationship, contrasting it with time and space relationships, with the relations of number and measure, and finally with our categories of ordinary causal relationships."[44]

Tremendum

The *numen,* although wholly other, manifests itself nonetheless as having a bipolar character. On the one hand, it is an object which is *tremendum,* and thereby generates boundless awe and wonder in him who experiences it. On the other, it is an object which is *fascinans,* entrancing and captivating the individual. The moment of awe and terror is, as it were, balanced by a simultaneous moment of longing and desire.

According to Otto there are three elements in the moment of *tremendum,* namely, awefulness, overpoweringness (*majestas*), and energy or urgency. The first of these is, for Otto, the starting point of the evolution of religion, or rather, in its antecedent form as "demonic dread" lies "the basic impulse underlying the entire process of religious evolution."[45] Demonic dread is later superseded by "more highly developed forms of the numinous emotion,"[46] but even where the concept of demon has reached the higher level of gods, "these gods still retain as *numina* something of the 'ghost' in the impress they make on the feelings of the worshipper, viz., the peculiar quality of the 'uncanny' and 'aweful,' which survives with the quality of exaltedness and sublimity or is symbolized by means of it. And this element, softened though it is, does not disappear even on the highest level of all, where the worship of God is at its purest."[47] The biblical concept of the wrath of Yahweh—the ὀργή θεοῦ—and the Hindu notion of *manyu*[48] are alike ideograms of this moment of awefulness. And although wrath later comes to be rationalized by terms arising out of the practical reason ("righteousness in requital, and punishment for moral transgression"[49]) Otto maintains that "something supra-rational throbs and gleams, palpable and visible in the 'wrath of God,' prompting to a sense of terror that no natural anger can arouse."[50]

The second aspect of *tremendum*, that of majesty or absolute overpoweringness, has as its subjective correlate "the feeling of one's own submergence, of being but 'dust and ashes' and nothingness."[51] It is in light of this that Otto takes Schleiermacher to task. In *The Christian Faith* Schleiermacher asserts that the essence of religion is to be found in the consciousness of being absolutely dependent, of being in such a relation with God.[52] According to Otto, Schleiermacher is enmeshed in a Kantian web, for (he wants to argue) Schleiermacher means in effect by "absolute dependence" a "consciousness of *being conditioned* (as effect by cause)."[53] That is to say, the relationship between God and the world is construed by Schleiermacher in terms of the category of cause and effect. I do not intend to suggest that the logic of Schleiermacher's "feeling of absolute dependence" leads to Otto's conclusion; indeed, Schleiermacher's theology can be seen as an attempt to avoid the Kantian critique. But it is useful to examine Otto's criticism of Schleiermacher, for it does give an insight into Otto's own theological position.

According to Otto, the difference between Schleiermacher's "feeling of absolute dependence" and, for example, the words of Abraham ("I am but dust and ashes") can be expressed as "that between the consciousness of createdness and the consciousness of creaturehood. In the one case you have the creature as the work of the divine creative act; in the other, impotence and general nothingness as against overpowering might, dust and ashes as against 'majesty.'"[54] The difference between the concepts of *createdness* (*Geschaffenheit*) and *creaturehood* (*Geschöpflichkeit*) resides in their respective views of the self. In "creaturehood" the self is seen as unreal, an illusion. In Schleiermacher, therefore, Otto wants to suggest, the feeling of absolute dependence entails "insistence upon the reality of the self."[55] By contrast, *majestas* leads to mysticism, to the ideas "first of the annihilation of the self, then, as its complement, of the transcendent as the sole and entire reality."[56]

The same comparison is used by Otto in *Mysticism East and West*, in a discussion of the Indian concept of *māyā*. There Otto sees the word "creature" (*Kreatur*) as capable of bearing two meanings: first, as a something brought into effect by the Creator, and therefore having existence and positive value in itself; second, as something pitiable, worthless, and a negation of reality and value. He argues, interpreting Eckhart and Shankara, that creatures have existence and value because, as creatures, they participate in goodness and being itself. Yet, insofar as they are apart from the divine, they neither exist nor have any positive value.[57] According to Otto, Schleiermacher has failed to perceive this negative aspect of creatureliness, an aspect that is apprehended nonrationally in the feeling of *majestas* and that finds expression in the mystical depreciation of the reality and value of the self and the world, because of his concentration on the positive value of the self and the creation. In short, Schleiermacher has emphasized the rational at the expense of the nonrational; he has failed to take proper account of the existential reaction to the apprehension of the *numen* as an absolute value in itself.

But theology can also err by overstressing the nonrational. By way of example, we can consider the notion that God is *exlex*. Otto writes, "Theology gives expression to its perplexed endeavor to find a name for the elements of the nonrational in the repulsive doctrine that God is *exlex* (outside the [moral] law), that good is good because God wills it, instead of that God wills it because it is good, a doctrine that results in attributing to God an absolutely fortuitous will, which would in fact turn him into a 'capricious despot.'"[58] He finds this doctrine in Luther, especially in his *De Servo Arbitrio*, the result of his debate with Erasmus on the freedom of the will. But he sees it as particularly characteristic of Islam as a consequence of the overstressing of the numinous element in Allah: "when Islam is criticized for giving a merely 'fortuitous' character to the claim of morality, as though the moral law were only valid through the chance caprice of the deity, the criticism is well justified."[59]

The notion that God is *exlex* does not appear to me to entail that God is the sole determinant of the moral law, since, as *exlex*, he is completely outside it; nor does God's being its sole determinant entail a capricious divine nature, for God will not *necessarily* act from whim or impulse, though there is the possibility that he may do so. Be that as it may, Otto's remarks are clearly directed at two issues. First, he wants to argue that the notion of God as capricious and whimsical is a poor ideogram, primarily because it puts the deity entirely beyond morality. For Otto it means that God would not be, could not be, a moral agent, and while (as we have seen) the idea of the Holy is not exhausted by its rational side, the latter is nonetheless crucial to it. Certainly, indifference to morality can be predicated on the nonrational nature of the *numen*,[60] but it must be construed negatively. This means that the illegitimacy of the notion of a fortuitous divine will resides not in the notion as such, but in its being taken as a conceptual affirmation of the divine nature, one which conflicts with the rational apprehension of deity as having a rational (and consequently not a capricious) nature.

In the second place, Otto is concerned to protect the autonomy of morality and thus, indirectly, the goodness of God. He wants to maintain that if morality is the result of the will of a capricious deity, then its absoluteness is destroyed. Moreover, it would entail the impossibility of attributing a moral nature to the divine, for such an attribution has meaning only if the morally good is determinable independent of God. To see morality as a product of the fortuitous will of God is to destroy the only basis upon which the attribution of moral goodness to God can be made.

Some of the subtlety of Otto's position is now perhaps a little more evident. He criticizes Schleiermacher's "feeling of absolute dependence" on the grounds that it fails to take sufficiently into account the nonrational side of the divine. In comparison, the notion of the divine will as capricious and whimsical fails to pay due deference to the rational side of the divine. The appropriate theology for Otto, then, will be one which stands like a coin on its edge, revealing both sides and not emphasizing one at the expense of the other. Of course, granting that there are two sides to the coin, there still remains a question: Why is the most appropriate kind of theology one which teeters on its edge? For there is no obvious reason why one side of the coin ought not to be better than its reverse. The logic of Otto's argument as a whole could be construed as favoring a claim that it is better to stress the nonrational than the rational, yet, as we shall see later, Otto does argue that a religion which harmoniously combines or incorporates both the rational and the nonrational is to be preferred.

Fascinans et Augustum

Although the mystery apprehended is *tremendum*, it is also, for him who encounters it, paradoxically *fascinans*, "a something that captivates and transports him with a strange ravishment, rising often enough to the pitch of dizzy intoxication; it is the Dionysiac element in the *numen*."[61] As such, it is the source of the quest for salvation and atonement, of self-surrender to the *numen*, of identification with it, of self-fulfillment in exaltation and ecstasy.[62] Its nature is best captured in Otto's own words:

> Widely various as these states are in themselves, yet they have this element in common, that in them the *mysterium* is experienced in its essential, positive, and specific character, as something that bestows upon man a beatitude beyond compare, but one whose real nature he can neither proclaim in speech nor conceive in thought, but may know only by a direct and living experience. It is a bliss which embraces all those blessings that are indicated or suggested in positive fashion by any "doctrine of salvation," and it quickens all of them through and through; but these do not exhaust it. Rather by its all-pervading, penetrating glow it makes of these very blessings more than the intellect can conceive in them or affirm of them.[63]

The *numen* experienced as *fascinans* is the subjective side of a further apprehension of it, namely, that it is *augustum*. As *fascinans*, it is recognized as of supreme value for man; but as *augustum* it is recognized as an objective value in itself. It is "august," writes Otto, "in so far as it is recognized as possessing in itself *objective* value that claims our homage."[64] The recognition of the objective value of the *numen* is accompanied by a corresponding devaluation of the self, and of existence in general.

This recognition of the *numen* as sacred, as *qādôsh* or *sanctus*, is central to the role of the category of the Holy in

Otto's thought. In *Das Heilige* it is clear that the sacred, that is, the Holy minus the rational elements, is a numinous category of value,[65] and that Otto wants to emphasize the difference between the complex category of the Holy, with its rational and nonrational connotations, and the purely nonrational category of the sacred.

Theologically expressed, the recognition of the objective value of the *numen* and the corresponding devaluation of the self is original sin or original guilt (*Urschuld*). The origin of the doctrine is the experience of the absolute unworth of the individual; its *locus classicus* is Isaiah 6. According to Otto, the God who turns his awefulness and majesty toward the world through his divine energy or urgency "is the true, the living and the jealous God, the God of high miraculous power, and God of flaming wrath and inconceivable grace. He is the God of action, in whom the *energicum* of the numinous is brought into high relief, forming indeed the special characteristic of that God."[66] In Isaiah's confession is expressed the realization of original guilt and an understanding of the mystery of all human existence. As such, Isaiah's experience typifies the universal existential status of humanity and of that moment of numinous self-devaluation in which it is realized. Otto writes:

> He makes this confession *not* by reason of any *theory* of original guilt, but from his own spontaneous feeling —it is an immediate, almost reflex expression of feeling with which theory has nothing to do. What he expresses is primarily the feeling of his own profanity, which keeps him apart from the godhead, and this not by reason of any individual transgressions, and not in any moral sense, but through his very nature as a creature and through his impurity in the religious sense, so that the godhead becomes unapproachable and untouchable and he himself stands in need of expiation and consecration.[67]

Sin, too, is explicable in terms of the character of the *numen* as *augustum*, for it is essentially the slighting of the *numen;* it is *superbia* "as the negligent or willful *opposite to humility.*"[68] The moral aspect of sin is neither its original nor its determining element; sin can exist independent of the morally wrong and even where the notion of gods is not clearly formed:

> Sin is a religious concept, not a moral one. The confusion of the religious concept of sin with moral offense has led to moralistic and juridical misinterpretations in Christian dogmatics which have obscured the actual sense and purpose of some Christian doctrines. If sin, transgression, lostness, deliverance from lostness, the Fall and inherited sin are pulled into the moralistic or even into the juristic sphere, to that extent they lose their original sense which lies wholly in the classical numinous sphere of the Old and New Testaments.[69]

Although the idea of sin is independent of morality, Otto nevertheless wants to maintain that, as the divine becomes rationalized (that is, conceptualized and moralized), so also the idea of sin necessarily combines with moral ideas—and this in a reciprocal way. For on the one hand, sin is perceived and recognized as wrong-doing; and on the other, wrong-doing becomes sin. "Immoral action becomes religious misdemeanor,"[70] although the sphere of the latter remains broader than that of the former. Sin remains therefore primarily infringement of the consciousness of the *numen* as *augustum,* though a consciousness which, when charged with corresponding rational ideas through the operation of the complex category of the Holy, becomes the Christian consciousness of wrong-doing, just as the august *numen* when charged with corresponding rational ideas becomes the moral law-giver.

Simultaneously with the realization of the valuelessness of the individual and the supreme value of the *numen* comes the awareness of the need for salvation, redemption, or atonement: "It amounts to a longing to transcend this sundering unworthiness, given with the self's existence as 'creature' and profane natural being."[71] The experience of salvation is the hallmark of a religion: "It [salvation] is something that does not in general allow of definition, that has to be religiously experienced, that is a qualitative and specific religious moment; a something that is experienced in nonsensuous and rapturous feelings. In that case, however, Buddhism is without doubt right from its beginning a religion."[72] Salvation marks Christianity out as a great world religion and, according to Otto, guarantees its equality with, if not its superiority over, the great religions of the East.[73]

The sense of the sacred, the consciousness of sin and guilt, the assurance of redemption, and the salvation consequent upon experience of the *numen*—these are the effects of the numinous experience. They are shot through with the apprehension of a meaning and value that is particularly and irreducibly religious. For Otto, the discovery of these fundamental elements completely determines the whole course of the history of religions.

The Evolution of Religion

Otto's interest in primitive religions was aroused by Wundt's *Völkerpsychologie*, one of numerous roughly contemporaneous attempts to give an account of the origin of religion and of its evolution. Likewise, in his discussion of the evolution of religion Otto was working within the context of the theories of Emile Durkheim, James Frazer, Andrew Lang, R. R. Marett, Wilhelm Schmidt, Edward Tylor, and others. He developed his ideas within the veritable epidemic of hypotheses proposed to account for the facts (or what were taken to be the facts) of the gradations and variations within religion—animism, fetishism, manism, totemism, polytheism, etc. Otto's account of religious origins and development must be seen very much within this context, and, like all these other attempts, it commits the fundamental error of depending on certain evolutionary assumptions for which no evidence had been or could be provided.[74] Still, Otto's account of the origin and development of religion is of interest, not for the light it throws on the *evolution* of religion, but as a reflection of his own *theory* of religion. His account is almost exclusively couched in terms which reflect and reinforce that theory.

According to Otto, both the rational and nonrational sides of the Holy are involved in a process of development. In the former case, although development fails to keep pace with that of the nonrational, the Divine increasingly attracts and appropriates meanings "derived from social and individual ideals of obligation, justice and goodness,"[75] and the Divine accordingly comes to have ethical content. But the more important task, Otto maintains, is tracing the development of the nonrational side of the Holy. There seem to be two central issues with which Otto is concerned: At what point in the history of religions do natural feelings (that is, feelings directed at a natural object) pass over into nonnatural and uniquely religious feelings? And at what point do uniquely religious feelings arise as the result of the apprehension of a transcendent *numen*? The issues are central because Otto wants to argue that the origin of religion is to be found at these transition points.

According to Otto, all the phenomena of primitive religion—notions of the clean and unclean, worship of the dead, magic, fairytales, myths, *orenda* or *mana*, demonism and polydemonism, etc.—share a common element: the feeling of the numinous. In other words, in all of these phenomena the category of the Holy is called into play. Yet here we are dealing not with religion in the proper sense, but with its predecessor; all these factors and elements (demonism aside) are "but, as it were, the vestibule at the threshold of the real religious feeling, an earliest stirring of the numinous consciousness."[76] Only with demonism does religion come onto the scene, for demons are products of the pure religious consciousness: "And in their case it is very evident that they do not arise as a collective product of crowd-imagination, and that they do not therefore have their origin in 'group'- or 'folk'-psychology, but were the intuitions of persons of innate prophetic powers. For there is always the *kāhin* (the primitive form of the 'prophet') belonging to these numina, and he alone experiences a numen or divine-demonic power at first hand."[77]

There are a number of reasons why these phenomena are not religious in the full sense. First, they display a realization of only part of the numinous; the element of *fascinans* is absent. And where the numinous is only incompletely presented, as in the case of demonic dread, too, there is "something bizarre, unintelligible, and even grotesque"[78] about it. Second, and more important, the numinous feeling is at this stage merged and confused with natural feelings. Numinous feelings may indeed receive their initial impetus from analogous natural feelings, according to what Otto calls "the Law of the Association of Feelings": "It [the numinous] is a content of feeling that is qualitatively *sui generis*, yet at the same time one that has numerous analogies with others, and therefore it and they may reciprocally excite or stimulate one another and cause one another to appear in the mind."[79]

Only when religious feeling is purified of the natural feelings by whose operation the numinous feeling is first awakened, and when it may be aroused independently of the stimulus and incitement caused by these, may religion be said to be present. Of the relations between the emotion of disgust at the "unclean" or the "impure" in a natural sense, and of religious "awe," Otto remarks, "when the more developed elements of 'awe' came upon the scene and went to shape the more elevated ideas of the demonic and the divine, *sacer* and *sanctus*, things could become 'unclean' or 'impure' in the numinous sense without any substratum of 'natural' impurity to serve as point of departure."[80] Thus, while natural feelings may be a source for the incitement of numinous ones, religion arises only when these latter are arousable independently of the former. No evidence is cited by Otto for the qualitative distinctiveness of these associated feelings, or for the passing of the one to the other. Rather, the qualitative distinctiveness of numinous feelings is a presupposition of his whole theory of religion. Once we have the key to the problem—the analogy of the two, and the law of the association of feelings—"we can construct a priori the actual genetic process involved, by which one emotion prompts the other."[81]

The third criterion for distinguishing religion from its prior phases is the apprehension in the former of a non-earthly object, in contrast to the latter's orientation to earthly objects. Again, it is the stage of demonic dread that is important for the evolution of religion, because here the religious emotion discovers the transcendent numinous object:

> The valuation prompted by the moment of numinous consciousness is attached in the first place and very naturally to objects, occurrences and entities falling within the workaday world of primitive experience, which prompt or give occasion to the stirring of numinous emotion by analogy and then direct it to themselves. . . . Only gradually, under pressure from the numinous feeling itself, are such connections subsequently "spiritualized" or ultimately altogether rejected, and not till then does the obscure content of the feeling, with its reference to absolute transcendent reality, come to light in all its integrity and self-subsistence.[82]

It is worth noting that Otto received criticism from both Protestant and Catholic quarters for his view that the primal apprehension of deity was of a nonrational and impersonal entity. Walter Baetke, for example, argued that the whole history of religions contradicted Otto's opinion, since universally in religions the nature of the deity is both personal and ethical.[83] And on the Catholic side Wilhelm

Schmidt, arguing from the standpoint of an original monotheism (*Urmonotheismus*), maintained that religion and
ethics were connected at the beginning and only later separated.[84] Still, Otto had no shortage of supporters. Two of the
most notable are Gustav Mensching and Gerardus van der
Leeuw. In his review of Wilhelm Baetke's *Das Heilige im
Germanischen*, Mensching concluded, "There is now no
doubt that in most religions, apart from the ritual domain,
the profane life of the community is also numinously determined and controlled, but the good in and for itself, moral
value . . . is no necessary element of religion."[85]

Whatever may be the historical relation of the religious
and the ethical, what is important for our purposes is the
fact that Otto's account of the development of religion proceeds on a priori grounds. His theory of religion is, as it
were, "verified" in his account of the generic origin of religion. Such "facts" as were available to him verified his theory, since they were interpreted in light of it. Clearly this
is a quite inadequate way of testing any hypothesis. Still,
Otto's technique is certainly no worse than any of the other
comparable theories in which finely spun webs of hypotheses appeared to be certified by the plethora of ethnographic
and anthropological data becoming increasingly available.
And his "verification" seems to have added credibility, in
some of his contemporaries' eyes at least, to his central
ideas of the uniqueness of religious feelings, the apprehension of *numina*, the operation of the category of the Holy,
and the nonrational autonomy of religion.

The Objectivity of Numinous Experience

Otto wants to maintain that in the numinous experience
there is the apprehension of a numinous object. This
means, first, that the feeling of something objectively present—the experience of a *numen praesens*—is part of the
phenomenology of the experience. At times he writes as if

he were arguing that the mere fact that the *numen* is felt *as* present is sufficient to guarantee the claim that it is present; he appears to suggest that religious knowledge can be gained merely by analyzing the nature of religious experience. He has been roundly criticized for his apparent subjectivism, for example, by Joseph Geyser in an early criticism of *Das Heilige*: "A feeling can certainly be focussed on an 'object outside of us.' But, that this object exists outside of us, we can conceive and think, but never feel."[86] Similarly, Baetke argues that Otto has not only generated a psychological impossibility but also committed a fundamental epistemological error.[87]

A number of factors make Otto's claim a much more interesting one and suggest that the claimed objectivity of the numinous experience is a more complex issue than it appeared to many of Otto's critics. First, as we saw at the beginning of this chapter, Otto emphasizes the qualitative uniqueness of religious feelings. We have since seen that religion in the fullest sense is evidenced where such feelings arise independent of any analogous feelings. Since for any feeling to arise there must be some source of stimulation, the only possible source is a nonnatural (that is, numinous) object. In other words, independently aroused unique nonrational feelings require a unique nonrational stimulus —the *numen*.

Second, the Holy is apprehended through the operation of an a priori category unique to it, which in its operation is a source of cognition. This is an aspect of the idealist philosophy that Otto derived from Fries. For Fries, the religio-aesthetic experience of *Ahndung* gives us positive knowledge of the noumenal realm and its relation to the phenomenal world; so also, for Otto, religious experience gives us positive knowledge of the numinous and, through the faculty of divination, its manifestations in the world. Numinous experience has, so to speak, a framework of Friesian metaphysics: "We employ the expression 'feeling of the supramundane' and thereby connect it to an old, traditional use of the word 'feeling' which is nonetheless quite definitely present in our language even today, e.g., if we speak of 'feeling of truth.' We mean here by 'feeling' not subjective states but an act of reason itself, a mode of knowing which is to be distinguished from the mode of knowing through the 'understanding.'"[88]

Third, the claimed objectivity of the numinous experience has a theological motif interwoven through it. Theologically expressed, the numinous experience is an experience of divine grace, a receiving of revelation. Indeed, in 1910, Otto concluded his critique of Wundt by saying that the psychology of religion and the history of religion would have to be a history of grace.[89] The numinous experience reveals the lack of value inherent in human existence by simultaneously revealing that which is of supreme value. Valuelessness is thereby overcome: "man, as a profane creature, resists the supernatural and keeps it at bay, and wins through only by means of a mystic act of rebirth which goes to the roots of his being, and which can come to pass only 'by means of the spirit.' In Christianity and Lutheranism these revolutionary phenomena find concrete expression in the doctrine of justification through grace in faith alone, apart from all works."[90] Faith is consequently that in man which makes possible the appropriation of grace; that is, "an independent faculty of knowledge, a mystical a priori element in the spirit of man, by which he receives and recognizes suprasensible truth, and in this respect identical with the 'Holy Spirit in the heart.'"[91] In short, faith and the category of the Holy are the respective theological and philosophical expressions of the means by which the action of the *numen*—grace—toward man is appropriated.

The objectivity of numinous experience receives phenomenological support in terms of the uniqueness of religious feelings. It is philosophically grounded in the cognitivity of religious feeling and theologically justified in the doctrine of justification by faith through grace. If there is any epistemological error involved, it is by no means a simple one. Otto's argument has many layers and needs to be evaluated accordingly. Because it is clear that the fulcrum of the whole argument is the notion of the category of the Holy, we must examine this notion much more closely in the next chapter.

Phenomenology or Philosophy?

The direction our study has taken thus far is perhaps sufficient to indicate that Otto is not primarily a phenomenologist of religion. First, I have suggested that Otto's claim that religious feelings are qualitatively unique arises not from the phenomenological analysis of the contents of the religious consciousness; rather, this analysis itself *depends* on the presupposition that those contents *are* unique. It is a presupposition, moreover, which is grounded in a philosophical theory to the effect that all religious feelings are the result of, on the one hand, the operation of the religious a priori, and, on the other, the apprehension through this a priori of a unique nonrational object capable of bringing them forth. Second, something similar must be said of the question of the varieties of religious experience. Otto himself does seem to recognize that there is a phenomenological difference between, say, an experience of demonic dread and the Buddhist experience of Nirvana; such phenomenological differences make it necessary for Otto to attempt an account of the origin and evolution of religious experiences. But that such experiences are, as it were, different species of the same genus, that they can be arranged in some kind of ascending order, is because there is a *unity* about them—a philosophically grounded unity, but not a phenomenologically discovered one. That all religious experiences are so many manifestations of the one unified mode of religious apprehension is a philosophical presupposition of their analysis, one which is grounded, in the final analysis, in Friesian metaphysics. Third, theologically, the variations and gradations of religious experience are also variations and gradations of revelation, for the numinous experience is, as we have seen, a mode of knowing: "Here I do not find but I have been found, I do not seek but I have been sought after, I do not discover, but I become enlightened. Here, I stand farthest removed from all 'phenomenology.'"[92]

All this is not to say that there are no phenomenological aspects to Otto's account, for while Otto clearly rejected any account of religion which would explain it in terms other than religious ones, he did not operate from criteria which were normative for any particular religious tradition. That is, he did not assume the falsity of all religious data or the truth of any particular set of data *as a methodological principle*. And he certainly saw himself as attempting to elucidate as fully as possible the meaning of such data for the believers and practitioners, at least with regard to their essentials:

> It is necessary to distinguish two distinct ways of approaching the whole question of religion, which are often confused. These are on the one hand the purely phenomenalist view, in which religion is treated as a 'phenomenon,' and as such is examined, as it were, from without, and is dealt with under categories which are themselves not religious. . . . On the other, is the method of approach from within, that is, from the standpoint of religion itself, which is practiced by the religious thinker, who uses categories that have arisen from the nature of religion. This we will call the theological.[93]

The analysis of religious experience as the apprehension of a *mysterium tremendum fascinans et augustum* is an insightful one, and a large number of religious phenomena can be interpreted in its terms. Moreover, as the breadth of examples in *Das Heilige* and in Otto's later work shows, it is enormously suggestive as a way of seeing parallels across religious traditions, and the distinction between *tremen-*

dum and *fascinans* captures a polarity that is present in many, especially the Semitic, traditions. As a heuristic tool, then, the notion of a *mysterium tremendum fascinans et augustum* is valuable. But without doubt, as a substantive account of the essence of religion, it remains firmly wedded to a philosophical theory. Edmund Husserl summed it up well in 1919. *Das Heilige,* he wrote,

> has impressed me greatly as hardly any other book has for years. . . . It is a first beginning for a phenome-nology of religion. . . . In a word—I cannot sympathize with the philosophical theorizing inserted. . . . The metaphysician (theologian) has, it seems to me, car-ried the phenomenologist Otto away on his wings. . . . Be that as it may, this book will retain an *abiding* place in the history of genuine philosophy of religion, or rather of phenomenology of religion.[94]

4
The Philosophy
of the Holy

Continuity and Discontinuity

In the last chapter we saw that, at a number of crucial points, Otto's phenomenological account of the nature of religious experience depended on certain philosophical presuppositions. The most important of these, for our present purposes, is that religion as a complex of rational and nonrational elements arises from "a category of interpretation and valuation peculiar to the sphere of religion,"[1] namely, the a priori category of the Holy or the religious a priori. Our aim in this chapter and the next will be to determine in more detail how this influences his account of the nature and history of religions.

An essential preliminary to this task is the resolution of the problem of the continuity of Otto's work—both within *Das Heilige* itself, and between it and Otto's earlier work. How we perceive his notion of the religious a priori depends upon whether we see an overall continuity or discontinuity within the corpus. It has been maintained, for instance, that there is a sharp break between the first part of *Das Heilige* and the more formal philosophical parts which begin (in the English translation) with Chapter 14.[2] The more the interpreter of Otto values the phenomenological analyses of the first thirteen chapters, the more inclined he is to see a discontinuity between the parts of the book in the transition from apparently phenomenological to philosophical concerns. Husserl is inclined to see the phenomenologist borne away by the metaphysician. And Theodor Häring writes, in a letter to Otto, shortly after the publication of *Das Heilige*, "the interpretation of the 'a priori' as a 'predisposition' in the Friesian sense seems to me independent of the acknowledgment of the value of your investigation of the numinous."[3] (He does go on to admit that he finds Otto's interpretation of the a priori clearer than Troeltsch's.) In a similar way, Paul Tillich remarks, "It now seems to me that the first half of the title [of this book] has been realized in an almost complete way, while with the second half a series of unresolved problems remain which demand further work."[4] Certainly, it has been the first part of the book that has guaranteed its place in the history of the science of religion.

Be that as it may, we must recognize that the explicit philosophy of religion in *Das Heilige* develops in a systematic fashion certain ideas alluded to or merely implied in the earlier parts of the work, ideas which subtly but significantly influence the apparently purely phenomenological account. Theodor Siegfried rightly points out that "the exposition of Otto is made too simplistic if the delicate feeling and literary power, the masterly skill of analysis and depth of vision are extolled, but the systematic conceptual content is passed over in silence."[5] Certainly Otto himself sees the conceptual aspects of *Das Heilige* as central to the book's purpose. Reflecting on it in 1932, he says:

> The subtitle of our book *Das Heilige* was: "concerning the nonrational in the idea of the divine." But the purpose of the book had been to a certain degree a "rational" one, namely, to restore to their rightful place the nonrational moments in the idea of God, and to bring them into the light, and *precisely* so. That is to say, to distinguish and to characterize them as far as possible in a rigorous analysis of feeling and through ideogrammatic symbolization, and thereby to draw near to the sphere of the rational, and at the same

time to show that they are the perimeter of clear rational moments which equally belong to the content of the idea of God. . . . Without these rational moments the "numen" would not be *God*, numinous value would not be the sacred, and quite certainly not the Holy of the Christian faith.[6]

Any claim that there is a radical discontinuity between *Das Heilige* and Otto's earlier work ought to be treated cautiously.[7] Certainly *Das Heilige* was startlingly fresh and exciting to many of its early readers, and it remains so still. But those who approached this book from a perspective informed by Otto's earlier work would clearly discern the continuity. Although there are developments and shifts in Otto's position at various times, the notion of a religious a priori is present, if only in embryo, in his earliest works.

In his edition of Schleiermacher's *Speeches on Religion*, Otto remarks that "the capacity for intuition and feeling is for him the religious a priori."[8] The notion of a religious a priori is also implicit in his assertion of the autonomy of religion in *Naturalism and Religion* and in his criticism of Wundt's *Völkerpsychologie*. As applied to the comparative study of religions, though, it becomes apparent for the first time in 1913, in Otto's lecture on the relation of Buddhism and Christianity. Of parallel developments in these two traditions, he writes, "Things which proceed so similarly in their historical development must be formed according to laws of parallel peculiar to them, must more or less originate in impulses of the human rational spirit, which are related to each other and belong in one category."[9] Shortly before this, a more theological expression of the religious a priori could be discerned in Otto's first publication in comparative religion. Again comparing Buddhism and Christianity, he concluded that religion "is a universal fact, and that it is not primarily dependent upon history but rather lives by its own divine strength and power."[10] Also in 1913, regarding parallel developments in Christianity and Hinduism, he suggests that they attest to "the inner unity of the religious impulse in humanity in general."[11] Moreover, as Friedrich Delekat reports, while at Göttingen (presumably the later part of Otto's time there) Otto was already lecturing on material which would subsequently be incorporated in a more developed form in *Das Heilige*.[12]

This is not to deny that there are differences between the religious a priori expounded in *Das Heilige* and the more general a priori suggested in Otto's work on Fries. And for some critics this was decisive.[13] According to the Friesian philosophy, knowledge of God, derived by the removal of temporal schematism from the category of community, is an aspect of the general a priori knowledge of human reason; so also with the knowledge of the rational side of the Holy. And religio-aesthetic experience (*Ahndung*) is, like numinous experience, a unique kind of experience; *Ahndung* is *formally* identical with numinous feeling, although materially different. There is a continuity at least to this extent. But while for Fries religion comprises an autonomous mode of apprehension, it contains no autonomous meaning or value; it serves merely to unite the realms of faith and knowledge. Here is clearly present a central feature of the discontinuity between *The Philosophy of Religion* and *Das Heilige*. In Otto's later work, religion consists not only of a unique form of experience but also of a completely autonomous religious a priori, an autonomous mode of interpretation and valuation. Thus, in the post-Friesian period, Otto's notion of the autonomy of religion reaches its fullest development. We can place the origins of this shift away from the Friesian position during or shortly after his engagement with the study of religions in their living contexts, that is, in late 1912 or early 1913.

In the transition to the adoption of a completely autonomous religious a priori, Otto came closer to the position of Ernst Troeltsch. As early as 1895 Troeltsch was a proponent of the autonomy of religion; for him, religion is "an autonomous sphere of life which develops and forms itself out of its own power."[14] Furthermore, in 1909 his notion of the autonomy of religion becomes formally expressed in terms of a religious a priori. Working on Kantian lines, Troeltsch wants to argue that the elements of universality and necessity in religion can only be accounted for in terms of a religious a priori; in so arguing he hopes to show how the subjectivism inherent in a merely psychological account of religion can be overcome, and thereby to enable religion to take its place alongside the other autonomous spheres of ethics and aesthetics.[15]

While Troeltsch's assertion of an independent religious a priori clearly predates Otto's, Troeltsch's influence on Otto should not be seen as decisive. Otto was aware of Troeltsch's thoughts on the subject, and in 1909 he even appears unsympathetic: "The problem of discovering the 'a priori religious'—to use once more this rather unfortunate phrase beset with misunderstandings—is now being approached from many sides."[16] Otto goes on to suggest that the dilemma of all such attempts was their failure to overcome Kantian subjectivism, the very reason why he himself had turned to Fries.

If Otto did move toward Troeltsch's position later, it was not because he was motivated by his discovery of Troeltsch's notion of a religious a priori. Rather, his trip in 1911 and 1912 and his subsequent involvement in the study of religions seems to me to be the decisive cause. Moreover, the position which Otto develops in *Das Heilige* is quite different from Troeltsch's. In the first place, Troeltsch's concept of the religious a priori is, in the final analysis, somewhat barren. As Ansgar Paus points out, "The actuality of such an independent category is more maintained than proved, is not made tangible, has no name and no specific content."[17] And Troeltsch himself seems to lose interest in it. As he turns more and more to the historical and sociological expressions of religion, the concept of the religious a priori appears less and less frequently in his work and finally disappears.[18] In contrast to the abstractness of Troeltsch's account, Otto's religious a priori has as its content the nonrational moments and rational ideas of religion which Otto generated from his examination of the religious consciousness, a method grounded in Friesianism. And because of this "filling in" of the a priori with rational and nonrational content, Troeltsch himself criticizes Otto's theory. He implies that it is in conflict with his own more Kantian position, and he clearly perceives its Friesian background: "This purely psychological and anthropological approach has nothing, or little, to do with the Kantian notion of the critical a priori, that is, the expression of an inner rational necessity and validity."[19] In short, while Otto moves towards Troeltsch's position in his assertion of an independent religious a priori, there remain important differences between their ideas. And while this move also signals the discontinuity between the earlier and later parts of Otto's work, there still remains a considerable amount of continuity which we shall now explore more fully.

The A Priori Category of the Holy

According to Otto, in the development of religion, the nonrational core of religion is progressively filled with rational and ethical meaning: "To get the full meaning of the word 'holy' . . . we must no longer understand by 'the holy' . . . the merely numinous in general, nor even the numinous at its own highest development; we must always understand by it the numinous completely permeated and saturated with elements signifying rationality, purpose, personality, morality."[20] Both the elements which go to make up the Holy are purely a priori. The Holy is "a combined complex category."[21]

We can turn first to the question of the rational a priori. Otto fails to develop this notion at any length, but if we interpret his statements in line with his Friesian background, we can obtain some measure of certainty as to what

he intends. Insofar as God has a rational nature, He can be
thought of by analogy with human nature. The content of
the rational a priori is determined by analogy to human nature, when the limitations imposed by reason on the attributes of human are removed and they are thought of as
completed, made absolute. The rational elements of deity
are consequently a priori because they can be generated in
Friesian manner by the completion of the analogous aspects
of human personality. They are derived not from any sensuous experience but from reason alone. The rational a priori
is analogous to Friesian *Glaube* "filled in," in this case, with
rational content. Only in terms of this Friesian framework
does the following passage assume clarity:

> The rational ideas of absoluteness, completion, neces-
> sity, and substantiality, and no less so those of the
> good as an objective value, objectively binding and
> valid, are not to be "evolved" from any sort of sense-
> perception. . . . Rather, seeking to account for the ideas
> in question, we are referred away from all sense-expe-
> rience back to an original and underivable capacity of
> the mind implanted in the "pure reason" indepen-
> dently of all perception.[22]

Also, with the nonrational element in the category of
the Holy, we are dealing with an a priori; in this case, one
which lies deeper in the self than the rational a priori and
which is "the ultimate and highest part of our nature."[23]
We are referred, writes Otto, "to that which mysticism has
rightly named the *fundus animae*, the 'bottom' or 'ground
of the soul' (*Seelengrund*)."[24] We shall return to this reference to mysticism in the next chapter, but for the moment
it is more important to note that Otto goes on to appeal to
the Kantian dictum: "But though all our knowledge begins
with experience, it by no means follows that all arises *out of*
experience."[25] Several paragraphs later he continues, "The
proof that in the numinous we have to do with purely

a priori cognitive elements is to be reached by introspection and a critical examination of reason such as Kant instituted."[26] Both of these passages raise the question of Otto's relation to Kantian philosophy, and a consideration of them should enable us to see the connection to the Kantian tradition much more clearly.

The appeal to Kant in the first passage above is not made specifically with reference to the Kantian notion of the a priori. The appeal to Kant at this point is essentially and only an affirmation of the basic Kantian doctrine of transcendental idealism; that is, that we can never know things as they are in themselves, but only things as they appear to us by virtue of the constitutive and determinative powers of our minds. The doctrine that the world of everyday experience is an "appearance" is fundamental to all of Otto's philosophical work.[27] In *Naturalism and Religion*, for example, he writes, "Kant shows us that if we were to take this world as it lies before us for the true reality, we should land in inextricable contradictions. These contradictions show that the true world itself cannot coincide with our thought and comprehension for in being itself, there can be no contradictions. Otherwise, it would not exist."[28] Otto wants to go further than Kant and, by means of the Friesian philosophy, to overcome Kant's dualism through the notions of *Glaube* and *Ahndung*. He aspires thereby to establish religion as valid, but its validity can only be established when it is shown that nothing counts decisively against the *possibility* of its validity. The basic doctrine of transcendental idealism provides just such a justification, for it guarantees that there is no necessary incompatibility between a religious and a scientific worldview; at the same time, it justifies the rejection of naturalistic and reductionist accounts of religion. In short, the appeal to Kant provides a foundation upon which an argument for the autonomous validity of religion can be constructed. It makes logically possible the claim that, though religion may have its point of origin in experience, it can only arise through the actualization of the universal human capacity for numinous experience. The numinous, Otto writes,

> issues from the deepest foundation of cognitive apprehension that the soul possesses, and, though it of course comes into being in and amid the sensory data and empirical material of the natural world and cannot anticipate or dispense with those, yet it does not arise *out of* them, but only *by their means*. They are the incitement, the stimulus, and the "occasion" for the numinous experience to become astir, and, in so doing, to begin . . . to be interfused and interwoven with the present world of sensuous experience, until, gradually becoming purer, it disengages itself from this and takes its stand in absolute contrast to it.[29]

Although the second passage referring to Kant in *Das Heilige*, quoted above, also gives the impression that Otto is working specifically on Kantian lines, the first edition of *Das Heilige* makes it clear that Otto has not Kant but Fries in mind. According to the first edition, the proof that numinous experience contains a priori elements is to be reached by "anthropological critique"[30]—a certain reference to Fries's anthropological method of introspective analysis. The expression is replaced by "introspection and a critical examination of reason such as Kant instituted" in later editions. In both cases, though, the meaning remains the same. Through introspective analysis, that is, through an anthropological examination of the contents of the religious consciousness, a realization of the qualitative uniqueness of religious feelings reveals their a priori nature: "We find, that is, involved in the numinous experience, beliefs and feelings qualitatively different from anything that 'natural' sense-perception is capable of giving us."[31] Otto's claim that in the numinous experience we are dealing with *cognitive* elements (*Erkenntnismomente*) is likewise a reflection of his Friesian background.

We can, then, discern a certain circularity in Otto's argument. On the one hand, he does imply that the qualitative uniqueness of religious feelings is due to their being evoked by a nonrational object, and, on the other, that their introspectively discerned qualitative uniqueness points to their cognitive character. Still, these aspects of the numinous experience—the qualitative uniqueness of religious feelings, their cognitive character, and their immediate connection to a nonrational object—do count against the argument that Otto's use of the term a priori is so wide "that there would hardly remain any mental phenomenon which was not a priori."[32] They *are* (purportedly) qualitatively unique and therefore a priori because, unlike other mental phenomena, they are related to the apprehension of a unique (because nonrational) object.

Both rational and nonrational a prioris guarantee for Otto the autonomy of religion, since they establish the necessity and validity of the religious a priori as an independent mode of interpretation, valuation, and cognition. In the cases of both the rational and nonrational a prioris, the incipient Kantian tradition is reflected through a Friesian prism.

Schematization

Although the nonrational elements in the religious a priori are the foundation of all religion, religion in the full sense is only present where rational and nonrational elements are intimately combined. As an apparent explanation of the relation of these elements, and of their union within the one category, Otto introduces the term *Schematizierung* (schematization). The rational elements of the Holy schematize the nonrational numinous elements.

Exactly what Otto intends by the use of this term is extremely difficult to ascertain. Virtually all commentators on *Das Heilige* agree that Otto's account is obscure and, as Bernard Häring points out, Otto's "theory of the 'schematization of the numinous by the rational-moral' has met with almost universal criticism."[33]

Otto first introduces the concept of schematization in his discussion of what he calls "the law of the association of feelings and ideas," a notion that, as we saw in Chapter 3, is important for his account of the evolution of religion. In some cases, he argues, the associations between feelings are "mere conjunctions or chance connections according to laws of purely external analogy,"[34] and consequently such associations are not permanent. However, we find religious feeling "in *permanent connection* with other feelings which are conjoined to it in accordance with this principle of association,"[35] a connection "according to principles of essential correspondence."[36] According to Otto, Kantian schematism rests on just such an essential correspondence. On the basis of an essential correspondence between the category and the temporal sequence, the latter schematizes the former. Otto concludes: "the relation of the rational to the nonrational element in the idea of the holy . . . is just such a one of 'schematization,' and the nonrational numinous fact, schematized by the rational concepts we have suggested above, yields us the complex category of 'holy' itself, richly charged and complete and in its fullest meaning."[37]

There is certainly an unexplained leap in Otto's argument: he moves from talk of the "association of ideas" and the "association of feelings" to that of an essential correspondence between ideas *and* feelings. Still, ignoring this hiatus, it seems clear that at the very least Otto is maintaining that the rational side of the Holy corresponds fundamentally with the nonrational side, not merely when each is taken as a whole, but also when they are considered according to the specific elements which comprise them. Thus, for example, he writes:

> The *tremendum*, the daunting and repelling moment of the numinous, is schematized by means of the rational ideas of justice, moral will, and the exclusion of

what is opposed to morality; and schematized thus, it becomes the holy "wrath of God," which Scripture and Christian preaching alike proclaim. The *fascinans*, the attracting and alluring moment of the numinous, is schematized by means of the ideas of goodness, mercy, love, and, so schematized, becomes all that we mean by Grace."[38]

These rational ideas must, in turn, be thought of as completed, as made absolute. As such, they are the correlates of the nonrational moment of *mysterium*: "The absolute exceeds our power to comprehend; the mysterious wholly eludes it. The absolute is that which surpasses the limits of our understanding, not through its actual qualitative character, for that is familiar to us, but through its formal character. The mysterious, on the other hand, is that which lies altogether outside what can be thought, and is, alike in form, quality, and essence, the utterly and 'wholly other.'"[39] "Schematization" means that there is an essential correspondence between rational and nonrational elements in the religious a priori, and that, since the nonrational is the core of religion, all religious doctrine can be seen as the result of an operation of the rational upon the nonrational.

How does the term *schematization* serve to illuminate it? And to what extent does Otto intend it to be understood in a Kantian sense? According to Kant, the pure categories of the understanding can legitimately be applied to the extent that they are brought under the a priori forms of intuition. In other words, they have objective validity only when they are schematized. For Kant, schematization is the means by which objects presented through the manifold senses are brought under the a priori categories. Because a schema is, so to say, nearer to sensible intuitions than the category, it makes possible the application of the category to the objects of experience. To use Otto's terms, for Kant, the nonrational schema schematizes the purely rational category.

If Otto were developing his concept of schematization

along Kantian lines, then schematization for Otto, as for Kant, would be the means by which the nonrational a priori might be applied to the object of the experience, that is, the *numen*. Although some commentators have suggested that Otto intends "schematization" to serve this function,[40] there are a number of reasons why this cannot be. First, Otto has no need to interpose a schema between the category of the Holy and its object. On Friesian grounds, Otto argues that knowledge of the object is *immediately* given in numinous experience. A *rational* schema (or, rather, rational ideas serving as schemas) clearly is an unlikely link between a nonrational feeling and its corresponding nonrational object. Second, whereas for Kant the nonrational schema schematizes the rational category, for Otto the reverse obtains: the rational elements schematize the nonrational. If Otto intends schematization as a means of apprehending the numinous object, then either he has misunderstood Kant, or he has illegitimately used the Kantian notion, or he intends to use "schematization" to serve another function. There is no reason to accept the first alternative, for Otto clearly understands what Kant meant by schematism.[41] Nor can he be said to illegitimately use the Kantian notion, since he needs no intermediary between the category of the Holy and the object apprehended through its operation. We must conclude then that he intends only a broad comparability between his notion and Kant's.

The key to the link between Otto and Kant resides in the *nature* of the object which is grasped by the respective schematized categories. For Kant, only a schematized category is capable of application to an object of sensuous experience. So also for Otto, only a schematized category is adequate to the elements of the divine. As we have noted, the divine object is the nonrational *numen* "completely permeated and saturated with elements signifying rationality, purpose, personality, morality."[42] Otto's purpose in using the term *schematization* is to assert that the relation between the rational and nonrational elements of religion is such that they are adequate to its object, and that the category of the Holy is adequate to its object, namely the nonrational *mysterium* and the rational absolute, and the characteristics pertaining to each. By *schematization*, therefore, we can conclude that Otto intends to emphasize the essential correspondence between the elements of the religious a priori and to assert that this essential correspondence and necessary connection of the two is demanded by the nature of that object to which they apply.

The necessary connection of the rational and nonrational elements in the category of the Holy is further reinforced by Otto's contention that "their inward and necessary union" is itself a priori. Of significance in his discussion of this a priori connection is its relationship to feeling. We can detect quite clearly Fries's notion of *Wahrheitsgefühl* (a "feeling of truth") underlying Otto's account. For instance, of the process by which the nonrational takes on rational elements, Otto remarks that it is "felt as something axiomatic, something whose inner necessity we feel to be self-evident."[43] In the first edition of *Das Heilige*, Otto argues that "the inward self-evidence of this process is in itself a problem which we cannot at all solve without accepting an obscure a priori knowledge of the necessity of the synthesis of these moments."[44] In later editions he maintains that the problem cannot be solved "without accepting an obscure 'synthetic a priori knowledge' of the essential correspondence of these moments."[45] The understanding of what Otto means by the a priori connection of these elements turns, then, on the nature of the problem which the assertion of this connection putatively solves.

In all editions Otto goes on to point out that the connection between the elements is not logically necessary; that is, it is synthetic, not analytic. The rational attributes of the divine do not entail logically its nonrational ones, and vice versa; the connection is between two logically unrelated areas. The problem consists, therefore, in the fact that the *felt certainty* demands a necessary (that is, a priori) connection between the two elements, whereas their respective natures point to their relationship as merely synthetic. To accommodate these two conflicting demands, the one entailed by feeling, the other by their logically unrelated natures, in later editions Otto maintains that we possess synthetic a priori knowledge of their essential connection. In other words, we know that these elements, although having a synthetic relationship with each other, are nonetheless *necessarily* connected. This is what Otto intended to say in the first edition, though it is clearer in its revised form. Be that as it may, the crucial aspect of the discussion is that the justification for the a priori connection of the elements *is the felt certainty of it.* It is crucial to Otto's whole theory of religion that the connection should be an a priori one, even if it is based on the somewhat light logical weight of a feeling of certainty. For only by an a priori connection of the two can Otto's claims that both the rational and nonrational are crucial to religion, and that all true religious doctrines manifest their intimate connection, be certified.

Numinous and Moral Value

There is also another kind of relation between rational and nonrational elements in the divine and the moral sphere. As we saw in Chapter 3, the *numen* is *augustum* and as such reveals itself as something not merely of value for us but also objectively valuable. In a 1936 edition of *Das Heilige,* Otto remarks that numinous value is "the nonrational ground and source of all possible objective values."[46] This notion of divine value as the ground and source of all objective values is only incipient in *Das Heilige,* but it is developed considerably in Otto's later writings on ethics and religion.[47] In these later writings Otto develops Fries's account of the nature of morality and its relation to religion. According to Fries, the categorical imperative is grounded in the immediate recognition and knowledge of value in the world; this value is itself a reflection of an *absolute* objective value. The complete autonomy of the Kantian moral imperative is limited in the Friesian account, for the moral imperative is grounded in something more ultimate, namely, the absolute value of Being itself, and the eternal purpose manifest in it.

Without putting too fine a point on it, we may say that for Otto the Kantian moral imperative is also grounded in objective values and rights. The objectively valuable, he writes, is "the ground of the validity of moral demand,"[48] and the moral ought "has its root in the basic right of the other person."[49] More important for our present purposes is the relation between objective values and rights and divine objective value.

In *Freiheit und Notwendigkeit*, Otto takes up Nicolai Hartmann's account of the antinomies between ethics and religion.[50] Of the five antinomies identified by Hartmann, the most incisive one for Otto is that between "autonomy of the good in and through itself, and theonomy, that is, the establishment of all 'laws' by God."[51] According to Hartmann, the antinomy resides in the fact that the essential autonomy of moral values is in contradiction to what is inherent in the nature of God, namely, that "in a world which is his thought and his value, nothing can be of value on any other ground, except that he wills it, that he commands it, or that it in some other way issues from his essence."[52]

Otto does not want to solve the antinomy by denying the autonomy of moral values, for there are autonomous values which, by their very nature, govern our conscience: "To offend the honor of another, to neglect oneself through lack of discipline, to choose falsehood instead of truth is in itself bad or evil, and what is evil ought not to exist."[53] Moreover, Otto wants to argue, even if we were to deny the complete autonomy of moral values, we are not thereby committed to the notion that "good is good because God wills it." He denies that the creative will of God could have created the world such that, for example, love would be evil and its opposite good.[54] A world of value could not be created by an arbitrary will, that is, by one which has no inherent value. Rather, far from being a capricious despot, God should be pictured as an "immeasurable self-dependent value-depth"[55] whose will is in itself good and holy.[56]

The assertion that the divine will is such is justified by numinous experience. The feeling of the sacred is that of something which has an objective value.[57] According to Otto, ethical theorists must take seriously the fact that this implies the deepening and broadening of values beyond the merely mundane sphere. Indeed, it implies the *subordination* of all mundane values to the transcendent value thus apprehended.

Furthermore, as a result of the operation of the *combined* religious a priori, the Holy is recognized as the *foundation of all values*. Otto writes:

> The feeling of sin and the feeling of the holy which obscurely implies and presupposes it is "the religious a priori" and particularly with reference to Christianity. Wherever the Christian message is explicitly present, there *the holy [der Heilige]*, the saving and redeeming God who judges sin and seeks the sinner steps into the light. Where this has happened, there is in all clarity no longer a mere teleology of all values in alignment with the holy *[das Heilige]*, but *the holy [der Heilige]* is the fundus, the ground of possibility, and the original source of all actual or possible value in the world and beyond it.[58]

Therefore, he argues, through the operation of the religious a priori we know that there is a congruence between the divine will and autonomous moral values. God creates a world interwoven with values that are reflections of his eternal and original value.[59] The will of God is a merely human expression for the element of absolute demand grounded in eternal value and reflected in the creature.[60] The autonomy of the creature is submerged in theonomy.[61]

In *Freiheit und Notwendigkeit* we can detect a development in Otto's view of the relation between the rational and the nonrational. In *Das Heilige* Otto asserts the necessary connection between the nonrational elements and the completed rational elements in the category of the Holy, and therefore in the divine itself. In his later writings, however, the relationship between the Holy and the sphere of moral values is twofold. The apprehension of the nonrational side of the divine (*das Heilige*) is coordinated with moral value, and the God who is both rational and nonrational (*der Heilige*) is the divine source and logical possibility of moral value.[62]

This does not entail Otto's denial of the autonomy of the moral sphere. It does have a certain logical autonomy, although its complete autonomy is nevertheless restricted. The apprehension through feeling of the dependent nature of moral value as a reflection of divine value does mean that the validity of the moral sphere does not rest on itself alone: "In the 'you ought' . . . sounds the original call of the divine for the awakening and aroused conscience: 'You ought to be holy, for I am holy. And, as holy and exclusively so, I alone am autonomous.' Here the last remnant of the supposed autonomy of reason withers away."[63]

Moreover, as the knowledge of the necessary connection in the divine between rational and nonrational elements is grounded in the felt certainty of it, so is the knowledge that moral value finds its source in the divine likewise grounded. The notion of the radiating of the divine original value into the creature is merely an "image" (one might say an "ideogram"), but one "which is not empty for our feeling of truth."[64] Such images, Otto suggests, do not illuminate the problem completely, but they nevertheless "let us sense [*ahnden*] something of its solution."[65] They hit on "something which is certain enough for us in our obscure feeling."[66]

Otto has not worked out anything like a complete account of the relationship between religion and ethics, and although the general thrust of his argument is plain, much about it is unclear.[67] For instance, he fails to make clear how a conflict between moral value and numinous value would be resolved, although he seems to recognize the possibility of such a conflict.[68] This, in turn, reflects the least coherent part of his argument, namely, that of the transition from numinous value as entailing the *subordination* of all mundane values, to divine (rational and nonrational) value as the *ground* and *source* of all objective value. The reasons for this differentiation are certainly not evident. Still, a transition of some sort *is* necessary, because Otto is in something of a conceptual dilemma. On the one hand, he cannot avoid maintaining that the numinous has a firm relation to value. His phenomenological analysis of the numinous experience shows it: the *numen* is, after all, *augustum*. And his account of sin and salvation depends upon it. On the other hand, he cannot maintain that the nonrational side of the divine is the ground and source of objective value, because the numinous is by definition nonmoral. Nor, perhaps unfortunately, can he argue that the rational element of the divine is such a source and ground, for this would entail the subordination of the nonrational numinous value to the rational side of the divine—a reversal of his central thesis. Consequently, somewhat arbitrarily, albeit somewhat consistently, he can only see objective value as grounded in the *combined* nonrational and rational Holy.

The Faculty of Divination

Through the operation of the religious a priori, the divine can be apprehended in the depths of the self. But the divine can also be encountered in the phenomenal realm. In the process by which religion arises historically, stimuli from the phenomenal realm, in interplay with man's predisposition for religion, actualize the latter. And by virtue of the actualized capacity for religion, that is, the religious a priori, aspects of the phenomenal realm may, in turn, be recognized as manifestations of the divine. There is, in short, both an inner and an outer apprehension of the Holy:

> Religion is convinced not only that the holy and sacred reality is attested by the inward voice of conscience and the religious consciousness, the "still, small voice" of the Spirit in the heart, by feeling, presentiment, and longing, but also that it may be directly encountered in particular occurrences and events, self-revealed in persons and displayed in actions, in a word, that beside the inner revelation from the Spirit there is an outward revelation of the divine nature.[69]

Otto calls the *faculty of divination* the means by which the Holy in its manifestations in the phenomenal realm is recognized and cognized; as such, it designates a capacity of the mind. It is a capacity to which theology bears witness by the expression *"testimonium Spiritus Sancti internum"* —"the inner testimony of the Holy Spirit." Otto wants to suggest that this expression can itself be divined as the only appropriate one "when the capacity of divination is itself grasped and appraised by divination."[70] In effect, it is the religious a priori which is active in the process of divination not merely as an inward receptive capacity but also as a productive faculty able to grasp the holy by pure contemplation, that is, "through the mind submitting itself unreservedly to a pure 'impression' of the object."[71] The faculty of divination enables a true recognition of the Holy in its manifestations through *anamnesis*, that is, through the "recollection" of its accord with that which is known *inwardly* by the operation of the religious a priori.

Divination is also grounded in feeling. Thus, for example, Otto maintains that what Schleiermacher is striving for in his *Speeches on Religion* is really the faculty or capacity of deeply absorbed *contemplation*, when confronted by the vast, living totality and reality of things as it is in nature and history. Wherever a mind is exposed in a spirit of absorbed submission to impressions of "the universe," it becomes capable . . . of experiencing "intuitions" and "feelings" of something that is, as it were, a sheer overplus, in addition to empirical reality.[72]

The doctrine of *Ahndung* as found in Fries and de Wette is also to be identified as resulting from the operation of the faculty of divination. We noted earlier that the content of *Ahndung* and of the numinous experience were, phenomenologically speaking, quite distinct. The experience of a *mysterium tremendum fascinans et augustum* bears, on the face of it, little analogy to the intuition of the Eternal in the temporal and the Infinite in the finite. Again, though, we may note that Otto maintains their formal identity because of their philosophical unity. The religious a priori, through the inward operation of which is apprehended a *mysterium*, is the same a priori which, when turned outward toward the world, apprehends the same divine in nature and history.

The capacity for divination is universal, but this potential is actualized in only a few: "it is only disclosed," writes Otto, "as a special endowment and equipment of particular gifted individuals."[73] Otto criticizes both Fries and Schleiermacher for underestimating the role which creative personalities play in religion,[74] and a similar element is implicit in his criticism of Wundt's derivation of religion from the processes of folk psychology.[75] Indeed, as early as 1902 Otto maintained that the new religion of Jesus arises from the depths of his own individual religious genius.[76] In *Das Heilige* such ideas are especially developed around the notion of the faculty of divination. A phenomenon in the history of religions—the role of unique individuals—is philosophically grounded. He writes, for instance: "The universal 'predisposition' is merely a faculty of *receptivity* and a *principle of judgment* and *acknowledgment*, not a capacity to produce the cognitions in question for oneself independently. This latter capacity is confined to those specially 'endowed.' And this 'endowment' is the universal disposition on a higher level and at a higher power, differing from it in quality as well as in degree."[77] This higher stage is the stage of the prophet.[78] The prophet is he to whom the *numen* has revealed himself, he who recognizes the reality behind its external appearance.[79]

According to Otto, there is even a third stage beyond the prophetic, one in which the supreme divining subject is also the object of divination par excellence. Otto finds just such a divinatory object in the central figure of Christianity. Although he sees him as its most perfect exemplar, Otto does not see Jesus as the sole representative of this type. Even at this point there seems to be a lack of exclusivism in Otto's thought, for which he has been criticized.[80] Otto writes: "the 'holy man' or the 'prophet' is from the outset . . . something more than a 'mere man.' He is the being of wonder and mystery, who somehow or other is felt to belong to the higher order of things, to the side of the numen itself. It is not that he himself teaches that he is such, but that he is experienced as such."[81] Otto maintains that Jesus was recognized as a manifestation of the Holy by the earliest Christian community,[82] and that he can still be recognized so today.[83] Whoever considers the history of Israel and Christ as its culmination cannot fail to recognize that Jesus is a manifestation of the Holy—but this as a result of feeling, not on rational grounds: "it is an immediate, underivable judgment of pure recognition, and it follows a premise that defies exposition and springs directly from an irreducible feeling of the truth [*Wahrheitsgefühl*]."[84] That Jesus is *one* manifestation of the Holy is a judgment which proceeds from the operation of the faculty of divination and the feeling of truth which accompanies it. But that Christ is the sum and climax of religious evolution is a judgment which proceeds from the fact that the religious a priori also provides a criterion by means of which the relative value of such manifestations can be determined. The task of the next chapter is to examine this function of the religious a priori.

5
The History and
Theology of Religions

Religion and Religions

As we saw in the last chapter, Otto wanted to argue that the complex of rational and nonrational elements that go to make up religion arises from the operation of an a priori category peculiar to it. Otto's most original contribution to the study of religion lies in his attempt to apply the principles contained in the concept of the religious a priori to the history and comparison of religions. This chapter examines Otto's major contributions to the history and comparison of religions in the light of the philosophy of religion which forms their foundation.

The relationship between religion in general and the specific phenomena of the various religious traditions is one of mutual interplay. On the one hand, the universality of the religious phenomenon, that is, that religion occurs at all times and in all places, is explained for Otto by the fact that the specific phenomena of religion are so many manifestations of the universal human capacity for religion. On the other hand, the recognition of the similarities between religions in their respective historical evolutions points toward the necessity of understanding them in a conceptually unified way, that is, of seeing them as so many manifestations of the operation of the religious a priori.

Because the specific phenomena of religion are manifestations of the religious a priori, it is possible to compare them. In other words, that they are *religious* phenomena and not merely disparate and unconnected facets of human existence is due to their being intimately and ineluctably related to the human mind's capacity to apprehend the Holy, that is, the religious a priori. The only means by which any religion can be understood *as a religion*, and in relation to other religions, is by its connection to that religious a priori by whose operation it came into effect. The religious a priori is, so to speak, the logical possibility for the study of religions. In order to understand Christianity, Otto argues, it is essential to view it in its relation to religion in general, and to other religions in particular.

The study of religions is not an end in itself. Rather, Otto sees it as a crucial part of Christian theology. As early as 1910 he maintained that Christianity could only be understood "in its natural affinity and connection with religion in general, i.e., against a background of comparative religion and the history of religion, to which the right approach is once more given by the philosophy of religion."[1] Even his translations of Indian texts are part of this theological program. Thus, for example, in the preface to *Vischnu-Nārāyana* he writes, "It will hopefully be perceived that the purpose of this book is not that of 'Indology' nor 'the history of religion' but . . . theology. It is as a theologian that I am interested in this religious form."[2] And of *Das Heilige* he later reflects, "Our line of inquiry in *Das Heilige* was directed toward Christian theology and not toward religious history or the psychology of religion."[3]

The history and comparison of religions has a theological purpose and is an essential prolegomenon to Christian theology. Furthermore, for Otto the history and comparison of religions is itself a theological exercise, at least to the extent that it is carried out in terms which arise out of religion itself. Theology and the history and comparison of religions meet in the analysis of the religious consciousness which has come into effect through the operation of the category of the Holy. The religious a priori is, so to speak, the "point of connection" between the Holy apprehended through its operation and the religions as the various expressions of this apprehension.

The religious a priori is not merely the reason why Christianity can be seen in the context of religion in general, or merely the possibility of the comparison of Christianity to other religions. It also functions as a means for the comparative *evaluation* of the different traditions. The relative value of religions can be measured according to the extent to which they actualize the religious a priori. The criteria for this evaluation are determined from "within" religion, that is, by the degree to which the Holy is *revealed* in each tradition. The religious a priori thus affords an "objective" standard against which its various manifestations can be measured; consequently, the history and comparison of religions can be a theology of religions.

While the religious a priori allows for the possibility of comparing religions, this latter in turn points toward the need to view religions as manifestations of such an a priori in operation. In 1912 Otto draws attention, albeit in an unsystematic way, to the parallels between Buddhism and Christianity and suggests that they are grounded in religious feeling. The religions of the East and the West, he writes, "are truly parallel, their similarities being now recognized as due to the working of an underlying power called in religious language, revelation, and in scientific language, common religious feeling."[4] In early 1913 the recognition of the similarities among religions in their historical development is presented more systematically in "Parallelen der Religionsentwicklung."[5] It would appear from this article that Otto's first realization of the parallels between religious traditions had occurred during his recent journey to India, for his contact with the Indian tradition of faith and grace (*bhakti*) seems to have stimulated him to develop the theme of the law of parallels in the development of religions, and its relation to the inner unity of the religious impulse in mankind.

According to Otto, four different kinds of parallel developments may be discerned in the history of religions. First, parallels which occur in "prereligion" appear everywhere at the beginning of cultural development—demonic fear, shamanic obsession, totemism, witchcraft, fetishism, and so on—and point "to a uniform and constant function of human psychology as the underlying determining factor."[6] There is a further parallel in the time at which the stages of prereligion make way for religion proper. In Greek culture this occurred, according to Otto, between 800 and 500 B.C.; the same period saw in the Far East the work of Confucius and Lao Tzu, in Israel the prophets, in Persia the reforms of Zoroaster, in India the development of Upanishadic doctrine and Buddhism, and in the West the teachings of Xenophanes, Parmenides, and Zeno. Third, along with this contemporaneity in time, Otto finds parallels in the nature of the religious ideas themselves. The concept of *Brahman*, for example, corresponds to the *Tao* of Lao Tzu and the *logos* of Heraclitus; later, the Christian mysticism of the West parallels the savior mysticism of the cults of Krishna and Rama. Finally, therefore, the similarities among traditions are so great, especially in the *bhakti* and Christian doctrines of salvation, that one can speak of a convergence of types: from quite different origins arise religious forms of extraordinary similarity. All of these parallels point to the universal religious capacity of mankind: "This law of parallels reveals one thing with compelling power: the underlying, uniform, and common capacity of mankind in general in East and West, South and North, which, because it is present and takes effect as a force of development, sets in process everywhere the formation of the religious life in conception and feeling, and which, because it is uniform, can produce such similarities in such various spheres."[7]

The recognition and analysis of these parallels in the development of religions is, for Otto, only a preliminary part of the history and comparison of religions. The finest task is the *contrasting* of religions in order to show whether one is decisively superior to the others and, if so, *how* this is to be shown.[8]

It is not part of our present task to explore the historical validity of Otto's suggestions regarding the parallels and convergences of type in the history of religions. Rather, it is sufficient for us to see that, for Otto, the parallels are due to the operation of the religious a priori and are evidence for it. The distinctive spirit of each religion is a result of the same process. With this in mind, let us now turn to Otto's two major works in the comparison of religions, his *Mysticism East and West* and *India's Religion of Grace and Christianity Compared and Contrasted.*

Mysticism East and West

Although Otto devotes a number of essays to the nature of mysticism in the period immediately after the publication of *Das Heilige*, his most important analysis is his comparison of the similarities and differences between the mysticism of the medieval German mystic Meister Eckhart and the Indian philosopher Shankara. His initial systematic engagement with the study of mysticism occurs from about 1916 onward. Such records as are available of Otto's library borrowings during this period suggest that, from 1916 to 1919, Otto was reading widely in the history and philosophy of mysticism.[9] Friedrich Heiler reports that Otto wrote to him in 1920 saying that Protestantism "would have to regain the pure mystical method,"[10] an aim to which we may see all Otto's works on mysticism as directed, despite the antipathy toward mysticism displayed by the leaders of the ruling neo-Orthodoxy. (Emil Brunner, for instance, praises *Mysticism East and West* as a piece of comparative religion; but his review nonetheless concludes that in spite of Otto's attempt to suggest the opposite, Christian faith knows nothing either of Indian mysticism or of Eckhart's.[11])

For Otto, the central feature of mysticism lies not in the nature of the connection to the divine, but in a specific idea of God. The term *mystical*, he writes, "is primarily a predicate for the idea of God itself, not for the relationship to the divine."[12] It is "experience of that which is mysterious, i.e., of that which steps out of the limits of the rational elements in the idea of God and constitutes its nonrational side."[13] In essence, mysticism is religious experience itself, with the nonrational numinous elements predominant. In the first edition of *Das Heilige* Otto writes, "As a provisional definition of mysticism, I would suggest that it is of the same nature as religion, but with a one-sided preponderance of its nonrational elements and, at the same time, an overstressing of them with respect to the rapturousness of the *numen*."[14] This means, of course, that there is in mysticism an ever-present tendency toward the rejection of the rational determination of the religious object. Thus, for example, of the speculation on "Being" in both Eckhart and Shankara he writes: "it becomes clear that for Eckhart as for Śankara the whole scheme of speculation about Being is in itself only a preliminary task, undertaken in the service of another and higher idea. In the light of this, Being itself takes on a new aspect. It is removed from the rational sphere to which it unquestionably belonged at first, and becomes simply an ideogram of the 'Wholly other,' of the 'Anyad,' the alienum, the dissimile."[15] Eckhart and Shankara are not primarily metaphysicians and mere speculative philosophers; both are motivated by the quest for salvation, for the realization of and participation in that which for them was truly valuable.[16] "Both are guided by their interest in something which lies outside scientific or metaphysical speculation. This idea measured by these or any other rational standards must appear utterly fantastic and completely 'irrational': it is the idea of 'salus,' of salvation, of *śreyas*, of *Heil*, and of how this is to be won."[17]

Through interpretation of the writings of Eckhart and Shankara, Otto attempts to discern two types of mystical experience which occur in both. These are designated as the Mysticism of Introspection (the Inward Way) and the Mysticism of Unifying Vision (the Outward Way). The former turns away from the world of external things and looks for the "real" within the inmost depths of the self; by contrast, the latter looks out upon the world of finitude and multiplicity and perceives the infinite in the finite, the eternal in the temporal, the unity beneath the apparent multiplicity.

According to Otto, three "logically" ascending steps can be discerned in the mysticism of unifying vision. In the first and lowest of these, the perceived world is transfigured in a unity in which space and time are transcended; all is one and one is all. Concurrent with this vision of the identity-in-difference of the world external to the mystic, the mystic realizes that he himself is part of this unity. The distinction between perceiver and perceived collapses. Otto quotes Plotinus to this effect: "He who has allowed the beauty of that world (seen in ideal unity) to penetrate his soul goes away no longer a mere observer. For the object perceived and the perceiving soul are no longer two things separated from one another, but the perceiving soul has (now) within itself the perceived object."[18]

Mystical intuition may remain at this stage, or it may progress to a higher level. While in the lowest stage the unity and multiplicity form a "coincidence of opposites" (*coincidentia oppositorum*), in the next stage emphasis is placed upon the Unity, conceptualized now as "the One." The One is the substantial, the permanent, and the constant beyond the changing and fleeting many; it is "the real value behind the many."[19] Otto is fairly obscure in his account of the relation of the One to the many, though a Kantian flavor can be detected. He appears to argue that, insofar as this relation can be spoken of at all, it may take either of two forms. First, where this stage of mystical intuition is grafted onto theism (here I take him to mean onto a rational notion of the divine), the One is called "God" and the relationship between God and the world is seen in causal terms. The indeterminable nonrational mystical intuition is combined with the rational absolute, and the doctrine of the transcendent creatorhood of God is generated.[20] Alternatively, where the nonrational remains predominant, the notion of immanence may be generated whereby the One "conditions" the many. "Conditions" is to be understood as an ideogram, and "'to condition' here means to lie at the basis of a thing as its principle, and to comprise it."[21]

If neither of these two ways of expressing the relation of the One to the many—the rational "causal" and the ideogrammatic "condition"—is taken as final, a transition to the third stage may occur. In this the One appears as the only truly real: "The many, at first identical with the One, comes into conflict with it, and disappears. It disappears either by sinking down into the invisible One, as with Eckhart, or by becoming the obscuring veil of the One, the illusion of *māyā* in *avidyā*, as with Śankara."[22] Again, Otto's exposition of this stage is a little unclear, perhaps because it is so succinct. Still, he appears to suggest that the two ways of expressing the second stage may be transcended by a further kind of expression in which, since only the One exists, a cosmic idealism may be generated as the most appropriate ideogram to express the nonrational nature of this kind of experience. The immanence of the One in things is transcended in the case of Shankara by the assertion of the sole existence of the Godhead; for Eckhart, although the One remains immanent, yet beyond the immanent One arises the completely transcendent One, "the silent void of the Godhead into which difference or multiplicity never entered."[23]

Schleiermacher's "feeling and intuition" and Fries's *Ahndung* are now seen as forms of this mysticism of unifying vision.[24] Otto thereby links Schleiermacher and Fries not only to mysticism in general but more particularly to the whole tradition of German mysticism. Certainly, in terms of their respective contents, the experiences to which Schleiermacher and Fries refer do seem to bear a closer analogy to the mystical experience of unifying vision than do some other examples of religious experience cited by Otto. He implies too that, like the experiences of Schleiermacher and Fries, the experience of unifying vision results from the operation of the faculty of divination.[25] This would certainly be consistent with his theory.

In contrast to the mysticism of unifying vision, the mysticism of introspection rejects the external world for the inward quest. For Eckhart, this inward quest leads to *das Gemüte*; for Shankara, to the *ātman*. Otto writes, "Both *ātman* and soul must free themselves from the world which surrounds them. They must withdraw from the senses and from sense-impressions, without attachments to the objects of sense; they must free themselves from all outward objects as well as from objects of thought, and thus from all manifoldness, multiplicity, and difference."[26] In the state so attained, the distinction between knower, known, and knowing is obliterated. For Eckhart, the soul "has become completely one and is the One."[27] Because the introspective state is one of undifferentiated unity, it may be seen as one in which union with or identity with the One is achieved. That which is realized through the outward way can be taken as identical with that realized inwardly.

Otto wants to argue that there is no *necessary* connection between what is apprehended in these two types of mystical experience. He recognizes, quite rightly, that if the introspective experience is spoken of as *entailing* the unification of God and the soul or as *entailing* the essential identity of the two, then it is impossible to account for those forms of mysticism in which concepts like God or the One are of minimal importance. He points out that the introspective experience may be conceptualized in, for instance, the nontheistic terms of the "system" of yoga: "We distinguish a *sa-iśvara* yoga and an *an-iśvara* yoga, i.e., a yoga with God and a yoga without God. That the latter cannot be a unio mystica with God is clear; but in the former also God and union with him is not the goal. There is here no effort after such a union, but after 'the isolation of the *ātman*' for which God is merely an aid."[28] Since the introspective mystical experience can be formulated without reference to the One, or to God, the "Godhead" of Eckhart and the *Brahman* of Shankara are not alternative names for the soul that has "realized itself" in the introspective experience. There is nothing logically necessary about the relation between the soul (or *ātman*) and the Godhead (or *Brahman*). Rather, the relationship between these is one of the synthesis of qualitatively different "entities."

Still, it is important to note that, according to Otto, the connection between the soul and the Godhead is an a priori one, for the mystic at least. The mystic "knows nothing of the two foldness of the ways, but from the peculiar quality of the objects he experiences both unfold clearly before him. He does not reflect on their difference. . . . It is to him an *immediately felt necessity*, and he has no need to analyze intellectually what is given as a certainty in feeling."[29] Like the a priori connection of the rational and nonrational elements in the Holy, the necessary connection between the soul and the Godhead is grounded in a feeling of truth, for the mystic at any rate. As a partial explanation, for the nonmystic, of the connection of the two types of mystical experience in a creative synthesis, Otto adverts again to the law of the association of feelings:

> What is for the mystic an essential and necessary connection of the two seems to us only a reciprocal attraction following the laws of psychology, e.g., the rule that in certain circumstances different, in other circumstances like experiences can intermingle in the soul under the compulsion of their resemblance, and can not only mingle together but in certain events can also arouse one another—*abyssus invocat abyssum*—can be the occasion of the wakening of each other, and in interpenetration can mutually enhance each other.[30]

What, then, are the resemblances between these two experiences which lead for the mystic (or, rather, for some mystics) to the assertion of their necessary connection? First, there is the nature of the soul itself. Soul and spirit are themselves numinous entities, "For however different it may be, on the one hand the discovery of the miraculous depths of the soul and God indwelling in the heart of man, and on the other the depth of the world in unity and oneness: both are above all experiences of *wonder*."[31] Further, the soul is a numinous entity because it is the divine image in man, or, rather, the image in man of the nonrational side of the divine: "For this divine image in man also does not merely consist in the fact that he is reasonable, moral, intelligent and a person, but primarily in the fact that in its profoundest depths his being is indeed for religious self-consciousness something numinous—that the soul is mystery and marvel."[32] Through the soul itself the vision of the divine unity of the world is attained.[33] The divine in man, as it were, makes possible the apprehension of the divine in the world. This means that what mystics call the "ground of the soul," the *fundus animae*, the "Synderesis," the "spark," or the "Inner Abyss" is identical with that universal human capacity to experience the numinous, that is, the nonrational religious a priori. Introspective mystical experience receives a philosophical explanation; at the same time, the nonrational a priori is validated by mystical theology. The facts of the numinous consciousness "point therefore . . . to a hidden substantive source from which religious ideas and feelings are formed which lies in the mind independently of sense-experience. . . . We call it the ground of the soul."[34] Because the ground of the soul is identical with the nonrational a priori, mysticism, or the capacity to experience mystically, is an essential element of the human spirit itself.

The similarities between Eckhart and Shankara arise primarily from their combining of the two types of mystical experience into a synthetic a priori unity, but Otto nonetheless finds substantial differences between them. First, there is Eckhart's emphasis on divine vitality, in contrast to Shankara's static conception of *Brahman*. The eternal "repose" of Eckhart's Godhead, writes Otto, "is both the principle and the conclusion of a mighty inward *movement*, of an eternal process of ever-flowing life."[35] There is in Eckhart also the assertion of a number of paradoxes quite impossible for Shankara, for whom they remain exclusive opposites: humility *and* identity with the divine, multiplicity *and* unity, activism *and* quietism.

Third, and most important, there is the difference between the ethical content of their teachings. This ethical difference consists in the nature of the value that is sought in salvation. It is the difference between apprehending the *numen* as *fascinans* and therefore as of subjective value, versus apprehending it as *augustum* and therefore as of objective value. According to Otto, Shankara emphasizes the former to the virtual exclusion of the latter; for Eckhart, the latter is of crucial importance.

> The evils which torment Śankara are the vexations of *samsāra*—wind, gall, slime, sickness, old age, endless rebirth, but not sin, unworthiness, unrighteousness. Yet these are the meaning of Eckhart's preaching and also of his mystical doctrine. . . . For Eckhart, too, the creature, as it exists in itself, is an object of suffering. . . . But right in the foreground of everything else, there is for him, something entirely different: namely, desire to win the "Esse" as *essential righteousness itself*, as the absolute objective value in contrast to the worthlessness of the mere *creatura, sicut est in se.*[36]

As such (and here Otto attempts to unite the mystical doctrines of Eckhart with the teachings of Luther) Eckhart's teachings are a mystical form of the doctrines of justification by faith and sanctification: "The *homo nobilis*, the *homo deo non unitus sed unus* (the man who is not united to but one with God) is also for Eckhart the *homo justificatus* (the man justified by faith)."[37] And, Otto wants to argue, the roots of this emphasis on the objective value of the *numen* are to be found in "the soil of Palestine."[38]

The crux of Otto's criticism of the Indian tradition, as

exemplified in this case by Shankara, is that it has a deficient concept of the Holy. The Indian tradition fails to take sufficient account of the ethical implications of the divine. Shankara's mysticism is amoral, for the eternal *Brahman* is itself beyond all good and evil. In contrast, Otto argues, the God of Eckhart is "the God of all moral ideas in personal purity and perfection and of the social commandment regarding man and his fellow creatures."[39] He later concludes, "Upon Indian soil there could never have developed this inward unceasing occupation with the soul's life as a life of *Gemüt* and of conscience, and therewith the *cura animarum* in the sense which is characteristic of, and essential to, Christianity from the earliest days."[40]

Already, then, in *Mysticism East and West* there is an intimation of those ideas of the relation between religion and ethics which Otto would more fully develop later. That is, he appears to suggest that the crucial difference between Christianity and Hinduism lies in the fact that, for the former, the Holy is the source and ground of all moral values.

Christianity and the Bhakti *Tradition*

In all his writings on the Indian religious traditions, Otto invariably emphasizes that Christianity possesses comparatively more developed concepts of holiness, sin, and salvation, and therefore a more developed sense of the Holy in general. This is especially true of his comparison between Christianity and India's *bhakti* tradition of faithful and loving devotion to savior beings.

In fact, Otto was a pioneer in Germany of the study of Indian *bhakti*. This is particularly true of his study of Rāmānuja's *Vishishtādvaita Vedānta*, a religious and philosophical tradition virtually unknown to German religious thought prior to Otto's engagement with it.[41] As Hans Rollmann puts it, "It fell to Rudolf Otto to introduce Vaiṣṇavism and Rāmānuja to a Germany in which Deussen's publications on Advaitavedānta had left theologians and historians of religion with the impression that this philosophical tradition was the only authoritative expression of India's philosophy."[42] That Otto was recognized as a seminal scholar in this field is indicated by the fact that he contributed the article on Rāmānuja to the second edition of *Die Religion in Geschichte und Gegenwart*.[43] At least until the end of the 1930s, German religious and theological circles placed a heavy reliance on Otto's assessment of Rāmānuja. To quote Rollmann again, "Otto is to be credited with having situated Rāmānuja's philosophy in its historical context and having dispelled the notion that the Vaiṣṇava thinker's religio-philosophical task was exhaustively explained by viewing his philosophy as an apologetic-theistic reflex to Śaṅkara's monistic challenge."[44]

The *bhakti* tradition appeared to Otto to be a more likely contender against Christianity than did the more abstract and speculative system of Shankara, though, to be sure, Otto recognized the significance of the theistic elements in the latter.[45] Christianity and the *bhakti* tradition are comparable because both are in essence doctrines of salvation that "put their questions as to the Absolute, the world, the soul, and God, only in order to develop the theme of salvation."[46] But their convergence in type is the most startling feature of their similarities. Otto writes: "In this Indian *bhakti*-religion there is presented, without doubt, a real, saving God, believed, received, and—can we doubt it?—experienced. And this is just why this religion appears to me to have been, and to be today, the most astonishing 'competitor,' to be taken seriously."[47] Indeed, according to Otto, there is a far-reaching agreement of Christianity with the *bhakti* tradition which even extends to those doctrines that seem characteristically Christian—"the doctrines of the hypostases, of the incarnation, the valuation of the 'word' as the proper source of religious knowledge, grace, election, strict exclusiveness towards other types, etc."[48]

Still, Otto maintains that the difference in spirit between

these two religions can be felt: "One *feels* that there the spirit of India breathes, here the different and, let us say at once, the incomparably more piercing and vigorous spirit of Palestine."[49] This difference in spirit is due to a shift in axis between the two religions; certain ideas central to the one are only fragmentary or partly lacking in the other.

In particular, a number of central and connected notions in Christianity are totally incompatible with the Indian tradition. Prime among these is the Christian doctrine of the Kingdom of God. Already in *Das Heilige* Otto had maintained that one of the central elements in the teaching of Jesus was the proclamation of the Kingdom of God. Christ's first and direct work and achievement "is the effectual bestowal of 'salvation' as future hope and present possession by arousing a faith in his God and in the Kingdom of God."[50] And the concept of Jesus as he who not only proclaims the coming Kingdom but also by his presence signals its advent is the central theme of his late work *The Kingdom of God and the Son of Man*. In this book Otto argues that Jesus was an eschatological and charismatic preacher whose person and work were part of an act of divine redemption which broke into history with his coming.[51]

Now Otto wants to argue that this kind of idea is completely contrary to Indian piety because the Indian tradition has a basic worldview incompatible with it. In the Indian context the world remains, according to Otto, "a *līlā*, a sport of the Deity, a concatenation without goal and end—true, not without objective existence, but eternally worthless, never arriving at a fullness of worth, never *glorified* and made an abode of the kingdom and of the final dominion of God himself."[52] Therefore there can be in Indian religions no real doctrine of creation, a doctrine which, he maintains, in Christianity derives from the idea that the world is destined to become the place of God in his kingdom.[53] Indeed, as early as 1913 Otto suggested that the decisive superiority of Christianity to Buddhism lay in its doctrine of creation: "God looked at everthing which he had made, and saw it was very good. . . . In the doctrine of the creation of the world through God lies religiously the decisive superior value of Christianity over the religion of the East."[54]

This negative evaluation of the world in Hinduism means, for Otto, that it can never aspire to be a fully ethical religion, for only by a positive evaluation of the world as is evident in Christianity can the world become the sphere of service to the Divine Will. Only when the divine is recognized both as the valuable in itself and as the ground and source of all mundane values can the Holy be said to be properly apprehended. Consequently, the Indian tradition fails to properly value the Holy as a complex of rational and nonrational elements.[55]

In essence, therefore, the axis of the two religions is quite different. Hinduism turns on the problem of how to escape from the world; *samsāra* demands a resolution in *moksha*. Christianity turns on the problem of the justification of the sinner in the world: "The God of the gospel is not one who rescues from the 'wheel of becoming'. . . . but one who seeks the sinner."[56]

Otto finds the similarities between Christianity and the *bhakti* tradition substantial, and the similarities between Eckhart and Shankara are also significant. Indeed, Otto's analysis of the two kinds of mysticism to be found in them has remained the (sometimes unrealized) foundation of a number of accounts of mystical experience. But it is necessary to issue a caveat with reference to the differences between Christianity and the Indian tradition. Hinduism and Christianity are extremely variegated traditions, and there are world-affirmers and world-deniers in both. The form of Christianity upon which Otto bases his account is undoubtedly one mediated through St. Paul and Luther. More important, though, is Otto's claim not only that Christianity and the other religions differ, but also that the former is of superior value. We need to consider more closely the philosophical grounds of this claim, but as a necessary preliminary we ought to inquire into the nature of the connection, for Otto, between mysticism and *bhakti*, or what he calls more generally *mystische Frömmigkeit* (mystical piety) and *gläubiges Frömmigkeit* (the piety of faith).

Mysticism and Faith

There is an almost universal tendency among English-speaking interpreters of Otto to distinguish between mystical and numinous experience as if they were two unique and distinct forms of religious experience, and to talk of the latter solely in terms of the encounter of an individual with a personal deity.[57] One would not want to deny that there is a phenomenological difference between, say, the experiences of an Isaiah and the experiences of an Eckhart; Otto, too, would recognize this. But he would want to argue that both the experience of an impersonal absolute and the encounter with a personal God are different forms of one experience, for all religious experiences are the result of the operation of a religious a priori and therefore (*pace* phenomenological variety) they have a philosophical unity.

In our earlier discussion we saw that Otto found mysticism to be an overstressing of the nonrational side of the Holy. Moreover, in passages in *Das Heilige* Otto points out the specific connections between various mystical notions and the elements of the numinous—*the mysterium, tremendum et fascinans*.[58] Mystical experience is clearly, for Otto, a form of numinous experience, that is, of religious experience in general.

The relationship between mysticism and faith, between the apprehension of an impersonal deity and union or identity with it, and the encounter with a personal Lord is most fully developed in an essay entitled "Mystische und gläubige Frömmigkeit."[59] In this essay Otto maintains that mysticism is always dependent on the nature of the tradition out of which it arises. Where mysticism, as it were, arches itself over a theistic foundation, there is an intimate

connection between it and more personal forms of theism.[60] Moreover, in mystical experience itself there is an
intensification of elements which are to be found in the
most simple forms of pious devotion. Faith as simple personal piety carries within itself mystical elements: "Already
in the most simple acts of real devotion lie moments
which, if they occur in an enhanced form, either directly
give rise to mystical occurrences, or are in such correspondence to these that they . . . can 'merge' into them."[61] An
absolute contrast between mysticism and faith is consequently impossible. Mystical experience as one of the nonrational depths of the numinous is, after all, presupposed by
the core of religion itself.

Further, the connection between mysticism and faith is
grounded in the object of religion. The Holy, by virtue of its
nonrational character, may be experienced as an impersonal
absolute; but, because the Holy has a rational nature, it can
be approached as a personal Lord. As we have seen, both of
these sides of the divine are essential aspects of Otto's conception of the Holy:

> It is often thought that the designations of deity in
> impersonal, neuter terms ("It") rather than in terms of
> person and masculine pronoun ("He," "Thou"), are too
> poor and too pale to gain a place in our Christian
> thought of God. But this is not always correct. Fre-
> quently such terms indicate the mysterious overplus
> of the nonrational and numinous that cannot enter
> our "concepts" because it is too great and too alien to
> them; . . . Assuredly God *is* for us "Thou" and a Per-
> son. But this personal character is that side of His na-
> ture which is turned manward—it is like a "Cape of
> Good Hope," jutting out from a mountain range
> which, as it recedes, is lost to view in the "tenebrae
> aeternae"—only to be expressed by the suspension of
> speech and the inspiration of sacred song.[62]

The connection between the personal and the impersonal
in the divine itself, a connection apprehended through feel-

ing in the operation of the religious a priori, makes for a twofold way of communion with the divine—the way of mysticism and the way of devotion—and for the intimate connection of the two. Faith and mysticism are, for Otto, two essential and necessary components of the religious life: "They are not different forms of religion, still less different stages in religion, the one higher and better than the other, but the two essentially united poles of a single fundamental mental attitude, the religious attitude."[63]

The Evaluation of Religions

For Otto, whether one is dealing with mysticism or faith, the difference between Christianity and the other religions lies in the former's more pronounced moral elements. And for him this entails its superiority: "We count this the very mark and criterion of a religion's high rank and superior value—that it should have no lack of conceptions about God. . . . Christianity not only possesses such conceptions but possesses them in unique clarity and abundance, and this is, though not the sole or even the chief, yet a very real sign of its superiority over religions of other forms and at other levels."[64] The grounds for Otto's claim that Christianity is superior arise from his determination of the nature of the religious a priori. The a priori category of the Holy provides an *objective* criterion by means of which the comparative value of religions can be assessed in two related ways.

First, the religious a priori is objective because religions can only be assessed in terms which derive from the analysis of religion itself, not from categories external to it. The religious a priori contains such terms: "The criterion of the value of a religion as a religion cannot ultimately be found in what it has done for culture, nor in its relation to the 'limits of the reason' or the 'limits of humanity' . . . nor in any of its external features. It can only be found in what is the innermost essence of religion, the idea of holiness as such, and in the degree of perfection with which any religion realizes this."[65] Second, it is objective because, in the operation of the religious a priori, there is a *real* apprehension of the Holy. That religion which most perfectly apprehends the rational and nonrational divine is the superior one.

The religious a priori provides a philosophically grounded objective criterion for the comparative assessment of religions, and this comparative assessment is at the same time a theological one. By virtue of the capacity of the religious a priori to cognize the divine object, the comparative assessment of religions is simultaneously an assessment of their value as revelation.[66] Because the history of religions reflects the unified process of development of the religious a priori the history of religions is a progressive revelation of the transcendent to the human mind.

The most valuable religion will be one in which there is the most intimate mutual interpenetration of the numinous with the most profound conceptual and ethical meaning. Christianity, Otto believes, fulfils this role most completely. His most important passage to this effect deserves to be quoted in full:

> By the continual living activity of its nonrational elements a religion is guarded from passing into "rationalism." By being steeped in and saturated with rational elements it is guarded from sinking into fanaticism or mere mysticality, or at least from persisting in these, and is qualified to become a religion for all civilized humanity. The degree in which both rational and nonrational elements are jointly present, united in healthy and lovely harmony, affords a criterion to measure the relative rank of religions—and one, too, that is specifically religious. Applying this criterion, we find that Christianity, in this as in other respects, stands out in complete superiority over all its sister religions.[67]

Two issues here need to be separated. The first hangs on the question whether the criterion thus developed is a valid one; the second, on the question whether it is Christianity which best fits this criterion. The first is relatively easy to answer, for it is clear from the direction our study has taken that the criterion developed by Otto coheres with the overall structure of his theory of religion. If the religious a priori apprehends the Holy as a complex combination of completed rational and nonrational elements, then that religion which most fully expresses the divine as consisting of such a combination is the superior one. To be sure, the validity of the criterion depends on the correctness of a host of factors which are part and parcel of Otto's theory—the nonrational as the core of religion, the theory of the evolution of religion, the religious a priori as a combined category, the philosophical unity of religious experiences, the cognitive status of religion, and so on. Should any of the elements which make up Otto's theory fail to be cogent (and we have seen reasons to doubt a good number of them), then the validity of the evaluative criterion is likewise in doubt. Still, and ignoring the questions of cogency, the evaluative criterion *is* compatible with the theory out of which it develops.

The second question is more difficult to resolve, for a number of reasons. In the first place, there is the problem of *how* to apply it. The criterion casts so wide a net that any number of religions might conceivably be adjudged to be caught in it. Certainly, as we saw earlier in this chapter, Otto does attempt to give detailed reasons why the Christian tradition has more profound rational elements than the other religions. But as he himself realizes, much depends on "feeling" and "intuition," on the cumulative effect of a large number of factors, and less on deductive reasoning. In the second place, there is the problem of deciding to what the criterion is being applied. Christianity is an extraordinarily complex and variegated tradition; as Otto himself points out, it has been at times completely rationalistic, and at other times it has overstressed the nonrational. So Otto is referring merely to an ideal form of Christianity or, perhaps more likely, to an ideal form of mystically tinged Lutheranism. In the third place, therefore, even if we were to admit its theoretical validity, Otto's application of it to Christianity is not persuasive.

One cannot but conclude that Otto's assertion of the superiority of Christianity is a judgment that proceeds from his own commitment to Christianity. That is, the Christian believer overpowers the philosophical theologian. Up to this point Otto thought about religion, and the relationship between religions, in a way unprejudiced (in principle) to the truth of any particular religion. At a number of points he affirms that he was always motivated by the desire to understand Christianity, but only in his application of the evaluative criterion to Christianity is he swayed by his own undoubted and deep personal piety. I believe he was aware that at this point he had left *Religionswissenschaft* behind and was speaking under the influence of his own Christian faith. And, after all, one would hardly expect a Christian theologian to find in favor of, say, Islam or Buddhism.

Let us remember, too, the theological context in which Otto was working. During that period the ruling theological orthodoxy saw the task of the determination of the relationship between Christianity and the other religions as, at worst, theologically improper or, at best, theologically irrelevant. Only in more recent times has Otto's theological method received some validation. Developing Christian awareness of other religions has led to much more theological reflection on the nature of Christianity's own religious heritage, to the recognition that elements of religious truth are enshrined in all world religions, and to the attempt to enrich Western Christianity by an absorption of Eastern spiritual values. To this extent Otto foreshadowed the modern theological awareness of other religions much more clearly than most of his theological contemporaries, and for that reason his work is of special interest to those who examine recent attempts to construct a Christian theology of religions.

Postscript

Above all, what is striking when one surveys the total extent of Otto's work is the breadth of concerns which he brought to bear on the question of the nature of religion and the establishment of its autonomy. As we have seen, there is a complex weaving together of numerous strands—psychological, phenomenological, philosophical, theological, and *religionswissenschaftlich*. The rich synthesis of these various strands makes Otto's theory of religion both unique and original.

I have tried to show in this study that the axis of this synthesis is Otto's philosophical theology. The whole theory revolves around the philosophical idealism that Otto derived from Fries, that he accepted early in his career, that he developed as a result of his ever-increasing engagement with the history and comparison of religions. In his mature Friesianism we find the point of connection between the phenomenological-psychological analysis of the religious consciousness and the theological intent which directed and motivated his work. The uniqueness of religious feelings, the nonrational core of religion, its rational analysis, the combining of rational and nonrational as the warp and woof of religion, the theory of the evolution of religion, the unity of religious experience—all of these bear an intimate relation to Otto's mature Friesianism. And it provides a transition, too, to theology. The feeling of truth and the objectivity of religious experience philosophically underpin a theology of revelation and grace. *Religionswissenschaft* with a Friesian foundation *is* theology.

Appendix 1
Aufsätze das Numinose betreffend: Table of Contents

Appendix 2
Das Gefühl des Überweltlichen (Sensus numinis): Table of Contents

Appendix 3
Sünde und Urschuld:
Table of Contents

Appendix 4
Religious Essays:
Table of Contents

I. Theology

II. Science of Religion

III. *Appendixes*

Notes

Chapter 1

1. James D. Smart, trans., *Revolutionary Theology in the Making* (London: Epworth Press, 1964), p. 47.

2. John W. Harvey, "Obituary for Rudolf Otto," *The Friend*, March 19, 1937, p. 258.

3. Heinrich Frick, "Rudolf Otto innerhalb der theologischen Situation," *Zeitschrift für Theologie und Kirche* 19 (1938): 14.

4. For a broad overview of Barth's developing view of nineteenth-century theology, see my "Karl Barth and Anthropocentric Theology," *Scottish Journal of Theology* 31 (1978): 435–47.

5. Rudolf Otto, *The Philosophy of Religion* (London: Williams and Norgate, 1931), p. 225.

6. See Ernst Benz, "Rudolf Otto als Theologe und Persönlichkeit," in his *Rudolf Ottos Bedeutung für die Religionswissenschaft und die Theologie Heute* (Leiden: Brill, 1971), pp. 32–33. This was also confirmed by Frau Dr. Ingeborg Schnack, a former student and close friend of Otto, in a conversation with me in Marburg on December 10, 1980.

7. Although Otto and Bultmann were colleagues and friends at Breslau, their relationship soured at Marburg. Bultmann, in fact, appears to have been singularly unimpressed by both the aims and the substance of Otto's scholarship. See, e.g., his letter to Otto on *Das Heilige*, April 6, 1918, in the Rudolf Otto Nachlass in the University Library at Marburg, 797/757 (hereafter cited as HS).

8. Joachim Wach, "Rudolf Otto und der Begriff des Heiligen," in *Deutsche Beiträge zur geistigen Überlieferung*, ed. Arnold Bergsträsser (Chicago: Henry Regnery, 1953), p. 201.

9. Schnack interview.

10. Ibid.; and also Frau Margarete Ottmer, Otto's niece, in a conversation with me in Marburg on December 7, 1980.

11. Schnack interview. Frau Dr. Schnack saw Otto almost daily during the last week of his life.

12. Ottmer interview; see also Frick, "Rudolf Otto," p. 9.

13. Quoted by Paul Seifert, *Die Religionsphilosophie bei Rudolf Otto* (Düsseldorf: G. H. Nolte Verlag, 1936), p. 1. See also Harnack's review of the eighth edition, *Deutsche Literaturzeitung* 45 (1924): 993.

14. See, e.g., Jack Boozer, "Rudolf Otto (1869–1937): Theologe und Religionswissenschaftler," in *Marburger Gelehrte in der ersten Hälfte des 20. Jahrhunderts*, ed. Ingeborg Schnack (Marburg: Historischen Kommission für Hessen, 1977), p. 368.

15. A. Barrett-Brown, review of *The Idea of the Holy* in *The Friend* 64, no. 8 (February 1924).

16. William Paton, review of *The Idea of the Holy* in *The Guardian*, May 21, 1925, p. 249. A recent accession of press cuttings (uncataloged at the time of this writing) in the University Library at Marburg, from the estate of the English translator John Harvey, indicated the almost universal acclaim with which his translation was received.

17. Apart from the materials contained in the Rudolf Otto Archive at the University of Marburg (hereafter cited as OA) and in the University Library, the most useful sources for the life of Otto are Boozer, "Rudolf Otto," pp. 362–82; Reinhard Schinzer, "Rudolf Otto—Entwurf einer Biographie," in Benz, *Rudolf Otto's Bedeutung*, pp. 1–29; and Rudolf Boeke, "Rudolf Otto, Leben und Werk," *Numen* 14 (1967): 130–43. A good summary in English is provided by Peter R. McKenzie, "Introduction to the Man," in Harold W. Turner, *Rudolf Otto: The Idea of the Holy* (Aberdeen: H. W. Turner, 1974), pp. 3–7.

18. Schinzer, "Rudolf Otto," p. 2.

19. OA989. He did, however, show a marked flair for languages. Paul Tillich later remarks that Otto had "an extraordinary gift for languages which made it possible for him not only to master almost all Western European languages, but to be also at home with Sanskrit, to read Russian, etc." (OA33).

20. Boeke, "Rudolf Otto," p. 131.

21. Ibid., p. 132.

22. Schinzer, "Rudolf Otto," p. 4.

23. See, e.g., Rudolf Otto, "Das Leere in der Baukunst des Islam" and "Das Numinose in buddhistischem Bildwerk," in

Aufsätze das Numinose betreffend (Stuttgart/Gotha: Verlag
Friedrich Andreas Perthes, 1923), pp. 108–13, 114–18, and *The
Idea of the Holy* (Oxford: Oxford University Press, 1958),
pp. 65–71. Surprisingly, Otto published nothing on Christian
art, though Benz reports that Otto gave many oral analyses of it
to his personal friends. See Ernst Benz, "Rudolf Otto in seiner
Bedeutung für die Erforschung der Kirchengeschichte,"
Zeitschrift für Kirchengeschichte 56 (1937): 396.

24. OA352, p. 16.

25. Ibid., pp. 21–22.

26. See, e.g., Otto, *The Idea of the Holy*, pp. 75, 89, 90–91.

27. Ibid., p. 166. See also pp. 190–91.

28. Otto, *The Philosophy of Religion*, p. 137n1. See also Otto,
The Idea of the Holy, p. 66.

29. OA352, p. 36.

30. In *The Philosophy of Religion*, p. 142, the original German edition of which was published in 1909, Otto includes the
sublime within the more general sphere of religion, and he remarks that this inclusion has never been seriously contro-
verted. In *The Idea of the Holy*, pp. 45–46, although the religious and sublime are recognized as closely related, they are
nonetheless seen as essentially independent of each other. See
also pp. 42, 62–63.

31. Rudolf Otto, *Die Anschauung vom Heiligen Geiste bei
Luther* (Göttingen: Vandenhoeck und Ruprecht, 1898).

32. F. D. E. Schleiermacher, *Über die Religion: Reden an die
Gebildeten unter ihren Verächtern* (Göttingen: Vandenhoeck
und Ruprecht, 1899).

33. Rudolf Otto, "Wie Schleiermacher die Religion wieder-
entdeckte," *Die christliche Welt* 17(1903): 506–12. English
translation: "How Schleiermacher Rediscovered the *Sensus
Numinis*," in *Religious Essays* (London: Oxford University
Press, 1931), pp. 68–77. Cf. also a somewhat altered version un-
der the title "Der neue Aufbruch des Sensus Numinis bei
Schleiermacher," in *Sünde und Urschuld* (München: C. H.
Beck, 1932), pp. 132–39.

34. Rudolf Otto, *Die historisch-kritische Auffassung vom
Leben und Wirken Jesu* (Göttingen: Vandenhoeck und
Ruprecht, 1901). English translation: *The Life and Ministry of
Jesus* (Chicago: Open Court, 1908).

35. Ottmer interview. Although Frau Ottmer believed that this occurred a little later in Otto's life, the most probable time was later in his period as a *Privatdozent*, when any future academic career was threatened by his exclusion from a full professorship.

36. Ernst Troeltsch to Rudolf Otto, November 17, 1904 (HS797/800).

37. Rudolf Otto, *Reich Gottes und Menschensohn* (München: C. H. Beck, 1934). English translation: *The Kingdom of God and the Son of Man* (Grand Rapids, Mich.: Zondervan Press, 1938).

38. Rudolf Otto, *Naturalistische und religiöse Weltansicht* (Tübingen: J. C. B. Mohr, 1904). English translation: *Naturalism and Religion* (London: Williams and Norgate, 1907).

39. Schinzer, "Rudolf Otto," p. 15.

40. Rudolf Otto, *Kantisch-Fries'sche Religionsphilosophie* (Tübingen: J. C. B. Mohr, 1909). English translation: *The Philosophy of Religion*.

41. See, e.g., Robert F. Davidson, *Rudolf Otto's Interpretation of Religion* (Princeton: Princeton University Press, 1947), p. 134n2. He reports that Otto explicitly affirmed his commitment to Friesianism in a conversation in 1923, and Schnack remarked that his lectures in the early 1920s were clearly Friesian in tone. See also Otto's notes on the English translation of *Kantisch-Fries'sche Religionsphilosophie* in Hans-Walter Schütte, *Religion und Christentum in der Theologie Rudolf Ottos* (Berlin: de Gruyter, 1969), p. 124, where Otto remarks that Friesian philosophy shows that the "theistic conception of a real and primal unity transcending the universe" is a fundamental element in our thought.

42. McKenzie, "Introduction," p. 4. The passage appeared originally in *Die christliche Welt* 25 (1911): 709. See also Benz, "Rudolf Otto," p. 36, and Otto, *The Idea of the Holy,* pp. 64–65.

43. Rudolf Otto, "Mythus und Religion in Wundt's *Völkerpsychologie,*" *Theologische Rundschau* 13 (1910): 251–75, 293–305. A revised version appears under the title "Der Sensus Numinis als geschichtlicher Ursprung der Religion," in *Das Gefühl des Überweltlichen (Sensus Numinis)* (München: C. H. Beck, 1932), pp. 11–57. English translation: "The Sensus Nu-

minis as the Historical Basis of Religion," *The Hibbert Journal* 30 (1931–32): 283–97, 415–30.

44. Schinzer, "Rudolf Otto," p. 18. See also Melford E. Spiro, *Buddhism and Society* (London: Allen and Unwin, 1970).

45. See, e.g., Rudolf Otto, "Über Zazen als Extrem des numinosen Irrationalen," in *Aufsätze*, pp. 119–32.

46. See Rudolf Otto, "Parallels in the Development of Religion East and West," *Transactions of the Asiatic Society of Japan* 40 (1912): 153–58.

47. See Martin Kraatz, "Die Religionskundliche Sammlung, eine Gründung Rudolf Ottos," in Schnack, ed., *Marburger Gelehrte*, pp. 382–89.

48. The collection is today a substantial and impressive legacy of Rudolf Otto. From 1947 until mid-1981 it was housed in the Marburg Castle. It is now in the newly restored Chancellory Building.

49. Otto, *Religious Essays*, p. 117.

50. See Rudolf Otto, "Religiöser Menschheitsbund neben politischem Völkerbund," *Die christliche Welt* 34 (1920): 133–35.

51. See Rudolf Otto, "Menschheitsbund Religiöser," in *Die Religion in Geschichte und Gegenwart*, 2nd ed. (Tübingen: J. C. B. Mohr, 1927–31), III, 2122–23.

52. Rudolf Otto, "Erstes Mitteilungsblatt des Religiösen Menschheitsbundes," 1923 (OA1162). See also Otto, *Religious Essays*, pp. 150–56.

53. OA1833.

54. It was in part revived in 1956 by Karl Küssner and Friedrich Heiler as the German Branch of the World League of Religions, and affiliated with the World Congress of Faiths established in 1936 by Francis Younghusband. See "Menschheitsbund, Religiöser," in *Die Religion in Geschichte und Gegenwart*, 3rd ed. (1957–62), IV, 876.

55. OA199, 200.

56. OA1194.

57. OA1202.

58. Friedrich Heiler, "Die Bedeutung Rudolf Ottos für die vergleichende Religionswissenschaft," in *Religionswissenschaft in neuer Sicht*, ed. Birger Forell, Heinrich Frick, and Friedrich Heiler (Marburg: N. G. Elwert, 1951), p. 17.

59. Rudolf Otto, *Dīpikā des Nivāsa: Eine indische Heilslehre* (Tübingen: J. C. B. Mohr, 1916).

60. Rudolf Otto, *Vischnu-Nārāyana: Texte zur indischen Gottesmystik* (Jena: E. Diederich, 1917).

61. Rudolf Otto, *Siddhānta des Rāmānuja: Ein Text zur indischen Gottesmystik* (Jena: E. Diederich, 1917).

62. Rudolf Otto, *Der Sang des Hehr-Erhabenen: Die Bhagavad-Gītā* (Stuttgart: W. Kohlhammer, 1935).

63. Rudolf Otto, *Die Urgestalt der Bhagavad-Gītā* (Tübingen: J. C. B. Mohr, 1934).

64. Rudolf Otto, *Die Lehrtraktate der Bhagavad-Gītā* (Tübingen: J. C. B. Mohr, 1935). All three of Otto's works on the *Bhagavad-Gītā* were combined into one volume for the English translation: *The Original Gītā: The Song of the Supreme Exalted One* (London: Allen and Unwin, 1939).

65. Rudolf Otto, *Die Kaṭha Upanishad* (Berlin: Alfred Töpelmann, 1936).

66. Dr. Martin Kraatz in a conversation on December 3, 1980, in the Rudolf Otto Archive in Marburg. But cf. Joachim Wach, "Rudolf Otto and the Idea of the Holy," in his *Types of Religious Experience* (Chicago: University of Chicago Press, 1951), p. 216. He describes *Die Kaṭha Upanishad* as "a model translation," though of course Wach was not an Indologist.

67. Rudolf Otto, *Das Heilige: Über das Irrationale in der Idee des Göttlichen und sein Verhältnis zum Rationalen* (Breslau: Trewendt und Granier, 1917).

68. Rudolf Otto, *West-Östliche Mystik: Vergleich und Unterscheidung zur Wesensdeutung* (Gotha: L. Klotz, 1926). English translation: *Mysticism East and West* (New York: Macmillan, 1932).

69. Ibid., p. 6.

70. Rudolf Otto, *Die Gnadenreligion Indiens und das Christentum* (Gotha: L. Klotz, 1930). English translation: *India's Religion of Grace and Christianity Compared and Contrasted* (London: S.C.M. Press, 1930).

71. These lectures appeared in English as Rudolf Otto, *Christianity and the Indian Religion of Grace* (Madras: Christian Literature Society for India, 1928).

72. Rudolf Otto, *Gottheit und Gottheiten der Arier* (Giessen: Alfred Töpelmann, 1932).

73. Rudolf Otto, *Das Gefühl des Überweltlichen*.

74. Otto, *Sünde und Urschuld*.

75. Otto, *Aufsätze*.

76. McKenzie, "Introduction," p. 6.

77. Rudolf Otto, "Wert, Würde und Recht" and "Wertgesetz und Autonomie," *Zeitschrift für Theologie und Kirche* 12 (1931): 1–67, 85–110; "Das Schuldgefühl und seine Implikationen" and "Das Gefühl der Verantwortlichkeit," *Zeitschrift für Religionspsychologie* 14 (1931): 1–19, 49–57, 109–36; "Pflicht und Neigung," *Kant-Studien* 37 (1932): 49–90. These have been collected and edited by Jack Boozer in *Aüfsatze zur Ethik* (München: C. H. Beck, 1979).

78. Rudolf Otto, *Freiheit und Notwendigkeit, ein Gespräch mit Nicolai Hartmann über Autonomie und Theonomie der Werte* (Tübingen: J. C. B. Mohr, 1940).

79. The date of Otto's death is variously given in the literature. His death certificate places it on March 6.

80. OA423; Ottmer interview. The details surrounding this event and its possible causes have not been published before. I do so with the permission of Frau Ottmer.

81. As both Ottmer and Schnack believe, though there appears to be no medical evidence supporting this. Frau Ottmer does recognize the possibility that Otto committed suicide. Frau Dr. Schnack, on "theological" grounds more than any other, discounts that possibility.

82. He was "depressive by nature" (Ottmer interview).

83. HS 797/178.

84. Ottmer interview.

85. Schnack interview. Frau Ottmer also remarked that Otto was dreadfully distressed by Jacobsohn's death, and by the fact that Otto was unable to adopt his son.

86. HS 797/170.

87. HS 797/171.

Chapter 2

1. Rudolf Otto, *The Idea of the Holy* (Oxford: Oxford University Press, 1958), p. 6.

2. Ibid., p. 4.

3. Ibid., p. 1.

4. Ibid., p. xxi. See also Otto's notes on the English translation of *Kantisch-Fries'sche Religionsphilosophie* in Hans-Walter Schütte, *Religion und Christentum in der Theologie Rudolf Ottos* (Berlin: de Gruyter, 1969), p. 123: "*On no account* do I wish to be considered a 'non-rationalist.' In all religion, and in my own religion, I indeed recognize the profundity of the nonrational factor; but this deepens my conviction that it is the duty of serious theology to win as much ground as it can for *Ratio* in this realm."

5. Rudolf Otto, *The Philosophy of Religion* (London: Williams and Norgate, 1931), p. 229.

6. Otto, *The Idea of the Holy*, p. 3.

7. His *Loci Theologici* (1610–22) are regarded as the epitome of Lutheran dogmatic theology.

8. Otto, *The Idea of the Holy*, p. 95. Otto buttresses this claim with passages from Plato's *Timaeus* (28c) and *Seventh Letter* (341c).

9. On Luther and the mystical tradition, see Otto, *The Idea of the Holy*, pp. 104, 204–7; also "Mystische und gläubige Frömmigkeit," in *Aufsätze das Numinose betreffend*, (Stuttgart/Gotha: Verlag Friedrich Andreas Perthes, 1923), pp. 71–107, and "Rettung aus Verlorenheit nach Luther. Justificatio per Fidem," in *Sünde und Urschuld* (München: C. H. Beck, 1932), pp. 43–60.

10. Otto, *The Idea of the Holy*, pp. 99–100. See also pp. 23–24.

11. Rudolf Otto, *Die Anschauung vom Heiligen Geiste bei Luther* (Göttingen: Vandenhoeck und Ruprecht, 1898), p. 15.

12. Ibid., p. 48.

13. Ibid., p. 53.

14. Ibid., p. 96.

15. Otto, *The Idea of the Holy*, p. 108. In Otto's own writings on liturgy and liturgical reform he stresses the desirability of a more contemplative form of worship in which the "real presence" of God may be fully and deeply experienced through a collective meditative silence. See, e.g., "Towards a Liturgical Reform,' in his *Religious Essays* (London: Oxford University Press, 1931), pp. 53–67, and "Schweigender Dienst," in *Aufsätze*, pp. 171–78.

16. Otto, *The Idea of the Holy*, p. 108.

17. Albrecht Ritschl, *Geschichte des Pietismus* (Bonn: Adolph Marcus, 1866), III, 195–438.

18. See, e.g., the epilogue, to F. D. E. Schleiermacher, *Über die Religion: Reden an die Gebildeten unter ihren Verächtern* (Göttingen: Vandenhoeck und Ruprecht, 1899), p. xxxii. Or perhaps earlier, for Otto himself possessed a copy of the first edition of Wilhelm Dilthey's *Leben Schleiermachers*, a gift from Dilthey.

19. Otto's review of Jakob Fries, *Wissen, Glaube und Ahndung*, ed. Leonard Nelson (Göttingen: Öffentliches Leben, 1905), in *Die christliche Welt* 22 (1908): 819.

20. In his review of Otto's *Kantisch-Fries'sche Religionsphilosophie*, in *Theologische Rundschau* 12 (1909): 424, Wilhelm Bousset remarks that Otto ought to have made more of Fries's connection to Moravian Pietism. He goes on to say that Fries's second wife was a member of the Brethren, as were his sisters.

21. Otto Uttendörfer, "Die Entwürfe Zinzendorfs zu seiner Religions-schrift," *Zeitschrift für Brüdergeschichte* 13 (1919): 64–98.

22. Rudolf Otto, "Zinzendorf über den 'Sensus Numinis,'" in *Aufsätze*, pp. 51–55.

23. Uttendörfer, "Die Entwürfe Zinzendorfs," p. 73. Cf. Otto, *The Idea of the Holy*, p. 113.

24. Rudolf Otto, "Zinzendorf als Entdecker des Sensus Numinis," in *Das Gefühl des Überweltlichen (Sensus Numinis)* (München: C. H. Beck, 1932), pp. 4–10. A revised version of his earlier essay on Schleiermacher's rediscovery of religion appears later in Otto, *Sünde und Urschuld*, pp. 123–39, under the (significantly) less emphatic title, "Der neue Aufbruch des Sensus Numinis bei Schleiermacher."

25. Otto, "Zinzendorf als Entdecker," pp. 5–6.

26. Ibid., pp. 9–10. See also Otto, *Sünde und Urschuld*, p. 139.

27. Otto, *Religious Essays*, pp. 68–69.

28. Ibid., p. 70.

29. Rudolf Otto, introduction to F. D. E. Schleiermacher, *On Religion: Speeches to Its Cultured Despisers* (New York: Harper & Row, 1958), p. ix. This is an abbreviated version of Otto's introduction to his 1899 edition of the *Reden*.

30. Ibid., p. viii.

31. Otto, *Religious Essays*, p. 71.

32. Ibid., p. 71.

33. Ibid., p. 77.

34. Karl Barth, *Protestant Theology in the Nineteenth Century* (London: S.C.M. Press, 1972), p. 266.

35. In much of what follows, I am especially indebted to Herbert J. Paton, *Kant's Metaphysics of Experience* (London: Allen and Unwin, 1936).

36. Norman Kemp Smith, *Immanuel Kant's Critique of Pure Reason* (London: Macmillan, 1964), pp. 41–42.

37. Paton, *Kant's Metaphysics*, I, 304.

38. Smith, *Immanuel Kant's Critique*, pp. 186–87.

39. Schleiermacher, *On Religion*, p. 31.

40. Otto, *Religious Essays*, p. 75. See also the introduction to Schleiermacher, *On Religion*, pp. 18–19.

41. Schleiermacher, *On Religion*, p. 36.

42. Ibid., p. 48. See also Otto, *The Idea of the Holy*, pp. 146, 171–72.

43. Schleiermacher, *On Religion*, pp. 214–17. See also Otto, *Sünde und Urschuld*, p. 135.

44. See Otto, *Religious Essays*, p. 112. Cf. Schleiermacher, *On Religion*, pp. 237–38.

45. Otto, *Religious Essays*, pp. 115–16. See also the epilogue to Schleiermacher, *Über die Religion*, pp. xxix.

46. See Schleiermacher, *On Religion*, pp. 241ff., epilogue to Schleiermacher, *Über die Religion*, pp. xxxi–xxxii, and Otto, *The Idea of the Holy*, pp. 177–78.

47. See, e.g., Paul Tillich, *Systematic Theology* (Herts: Nisbet, 1968), I, 47; Richard R. Niebuhr, *Schleiermacher on Christ and Religion* (London: S.C.M. Press, 1964), pp. 116–17; Robert R. Williams, *Schleiermacher the Theologian* (Philadelphia: Fortress Press, 1978).

48. Introduction to Schleiermacher, *On Religion*, p. xix. See also epilogue to Schleiermacher, *Über die Religion*, pp. xxxii–xxxiii.

49. Epilogue to Schleiermacher, *Über die Religion*, p. xviii. See also Schleiermacher, *On Religion*, pp. 21, 71, 278.

50. Introduction to Schleiermacher, *On Religion*, p. xix.

51. Ibid., p. xii. See also Otto, *The Philosophy of Religion*, p. 23.

52. Rudolf Otto, *Naturalism and Religion* (London: Williams and Norgate, 1907), p. 76.

53. Otto, *The Philosophy of Religion*, p. 15.

54. Ibid., p. 23.

55. Otto, *Naturalism and Religion*, pp. 5–6.

56. Ibid., p. 7.

57. Ibid., p. 42.

58. Ibid., p. 41. On dependence, see also pp. 64–65, 55, 58; Otto, *Religious Essays*, p. 137; and cf. Otto, *The Idea of the Holy*, pp. 9–10, 20, 108. On mystery, see Otto, *Naturalism and Religion*, p. 53, and, on purpose, pp. 151, 80, 82, 129.

59. Otto, *The Philosophy of Religion*, p. 49.

60. It is interesting to note that Schleiermacher voted for Hegel rather than for Fries to replace Johann G. Fichte in the chair of philosophy at Berlin. At the least, then, Schleiermacher did not see Fries as the best speculative philosopher available, despite the compatibility of their ideas, and much to the annoyance of Fries's disciple and Schleiermacher's friend and colleague Wilhelm de Wette. See Richard Crouter, "Hegel and Schleiermacher at Berlin: A Many-Sided Debate," *Journal of the American Academy of Religion* 48 (1980): 27–29. I am grateful to Dr. John Clayton for this reference. See also Otto, *The Philosophy of Religion*, pp. 26–27.

61. See Robert Morgan, *Ernst Troeltsch: Writings on Theology and Religion* (London: Duckworth, 1977), p. 13.

62. Ibid., p. 13.

63. Ibid., p. 87.

64. Jakob F. Fries, *Wissen, Glaube und Ahndung* (Göttingen: Öffentliches Leben, 1931), pp. 63–64.

65. Ibid., pp. 19–30.

66. See ibid., p. 35.

67. Ibid., p. 29.

68. Otto, *The Philosophy of Religion*, pp. 53, 58–59.

69. Ibid., p. 78.

70. Robert F. Davidson, *Rudolf Otto's Interpretation of Religion* (Princeton: Princeton University Press, 1947), p. 144. See also Otto, *The Philosophy of Religion*, pp. 66–67, 81.

71. Otto, *The Philosophy of Religion*, pp. 84–85.

72. Ibid., p. 85.

73. Ibid., p. 87.

74. See ibid., pp. 99–100. See also Fries, *Wissen, Glaube und Ahndung*, p. 122.

75. Otto, *The Philosophy of Religion*, p. 115.

76. Ibid., pp. 123–24. See also Fries, *Wissen, Glaube und Ahndung*, pp. 143–47.

77. Fries, *Wissen, Glaube und Ahndung*, p. 175.

78. *Ahndung* is somewhat archaic for what was in Otto's time and is today rendered by *Ahnung*; similarly with the verbal cognates *ahnden* and *ahnen*. In *The Philosophy of Religion* Otto uses *Ahnung* and its cognate. In *Das Heilige* and *Mysticism East and West*, for example, he reverts to *Ahndung*.

79. Otto, *The Philosophy of Religion*, pp. 100–101. See also pp. 141–44.

80. Fries, *Wissen, Glaube und Ahndung*, p. 235.

81. Otto, *The Philosophy of Religion*, p. 133.

82. See Otto, *The Idea of the Holy*, pp. 145–47.

83. Otto, *The Philosophy of Religion*, p. 224.

84. Ibid., p. 224.

Chapter 3

1. Rudolf Otto, *The Idea of the Holy* (Oxford: Oxford University Press, 1958), p. 1.

2. Ibid., p. 59.

3. Ibid., p. 1.

4. Ibid.

5. Rudolf Otto, *Das Heilige* (Breslau: Trewendt und Granier, 1917), p. 2.

6. Otto, *The Idea of the Holy*, pp. 58–59.

7. Ibid., p. 59. See also Rudolf Otto, *Gottheit und Gottheiten der Arier* (Giessen: Alfred Töpelmann, 1932), p. 4.

8. Otto, *The Idea of the Holy*, p. 5.

9. David Bastow, "Otto and Numinous Experience," *Religious Studies* 12 (1976): 165.

10. Otto, *The Idea of the Holy*, p. 6.

11. Ibid., pp. 6–7.

12. Rudolf Otto, *Das Gefühl des Überweltlichen (Sensus Numinis)* (München: C. H. Beck, 1932), pp. 1–2. See also p. 7.

13. See Joachim Ritter, *Historisches Wörterbuch der Philosophie* (Basel/Stuttgart: Schwabe, 1974), III, 1034–37.

14. Thus, e.g., Fries says that the "absolute unity in the eternal being of things" is holy. See Paul Seifert, *Die Religionsphilosophie bei Rudolf Otto*, (Düsseldorf: G. H. Nolte Verlag, 1936), pp. 24–26. And de Wette remarks that "The Holy is however higher than the Beautiful and Christianity directs us to this." See Ansgar Paus, *Religiöser Erkenntnisgrund: Herkunft und Wesen der Aprioritheorie Rudolf Ottos* (Leiden: Brill, 1966), p. 114.

15. See, e.g., Robert F. Davidson, *Rudolf Otto's Interpretation of Religion* (Princeton: Princeton University Press, 1947); Paus, *Religiöser Erkenntnisgrund*, p. 111n79; Ernst Troeltsch, "Zur Religionsphilosophie," *Kant-Studien* 23 (1919): 65.

16. The essay appears in English in the chapter entitled "Religious Problems" in Wilhelm Windelband, *An Introduction to Philosophy* (London: T. Fischer Unwin, 1921).

17. Ibid., p. 324.

18. Ibid., p. 326.

19. Nathan Söderblom, *Gudstrons uppkommst* (Stockholm: H. Geber, 1914). German translation: *Das Werden des Gottesglaubens* (Leipzig: R. Stübe, 1916).

20. Nathan Söderblom, "Holiness," in *Encyclopaedia of Religion and Ethics*, ed. James Hastings (Edinburgh: T. and T. Clark, 1913), VI, 731.

21. Rudolf Otto, "Parallelen und Wertunterschiede im Christentum und Buddatum," OA351, pp. 23–24. See also his *Mysticism East and West* (New York: Macmillan, 1932), p. 160.

22. Söderblom, "Holiness," p. 731. See also Söderblom, *Das Werden*, p. 181.

23. Söderblom, "Holiness," p. 732.

24. See also Otto, *The Idea of the Holy*, p. 15n1.

25. Rudolf Otto, review of Söderblom, *Gudstrons uppkommst*, in *Theologische Literaturzeitung* 40 (1915): 4. See also Otto, *The Idea of the Holy*, pp. 74–75.

26. Otto, *The Idea of the Holy*, p. 15n1.

27. Rudolf Otto, "The Sensus Numinis as the Historical Basis of Religion," *The Hibbert Journal* 30 (1931–32): 427.

28. Rudolf Otto, "Mythus und Religion in Wundt's *Völkerpsychologie*," *Theologische Rundschau* 13 (1910): 301. Otto's first use of the term *numen* is in *Die Anschauung vom Heiligen Geiste bei Luther* (Göttingen: Vandenhoeck und Ruprecht, 1898), pp. 99, 100.

29. Otto, "Mythus und Religion," p. 303.

30. Ibid., pp. 304–5.

31. Ibid., p. 297.

32. Ibid., p. 304.

33. Otto, *The Idea of the Holy*, p. 60.

34. Ibid., p. 13. See also pp. 30, 39.

35. Ibid., p. 8. See also p. 224 and Rudolf Otto, *Sünde und Urschuld* (München: C. H. Beck, 1932), p. 139.

36. Otto, *The Idea of the Holy*, p. 91. See also Rudolf Otto, *Freiheit und Notwendigkeit, ein Gespräch mit Nicolai Hartmann über Autonomie und Theonomie der Werte* (Tübingen: J. C. B. Mohr, 1940), p. 5.

37. Otto, *The Idea of the Holy*, p. 26.

38. Ibid.

39. Seifert, *Die Religionsphilosophie*, pp. 26–27. It is interesting to note that both Barth and Otto speak of God as *das ganz Andere*. Barth's source for this phrase is undoubtedly Søren Kierkegaard. Otto's use of it has overtones of Kierkegaard also, but I have found no evidence that Otto was at all familiar with Kierkegaard's works.

40. Bernhard Häring, "'Das Heilige' Rudolf Ottos in der neueren Kritik," *Geist und Leben* 24 (1951): 71. See also Otto, *Das Gefühl des Überweltlichen*, p. 266; cf. Otto, *The Idea of the Holy*, p. 197.

41. Otto, *The Idea of the Holy*, p. 184.

42. Rudolf Otto, *Religious Essays* (London: Oxford University Press, 1931), p. 83.

43. Ibid., p. 87.

44. Ibid., p. 85.

45. Otto, *The Idea of the Holy*, p. 15.

46. Ibid., p. 16.

47. Ibid., p. 17.

48. Otto, *Gottheit und Gottheiten*, p. 9. See also Otto, *Das Gefühl des Überweltlichen*, pp. 123–24.

49. Otto, *The Idea of the Holy*, p. 19.

50. Ibid.

51. Ibid., p. 20.

52. See F. D. E. Schleiermacher, *The Christian Faith* (Edinburgh: T. and T. Clark, 1928), pp. 12ff.

53. Otto, *The Idea of the Holy*, p. 20.

54. Ibid., pp. 20–21.

55. Ibid., p. 21.

56. Ibid.

57. Otto, *Mysticism East and West*, p. 115.

58. Otto, *The Idea of the Holy*, p. 101.

59. Ibid., pp. 90–91.

60. Ibid., p. 107.

61. Ibid., p. 31.

62. See ibid., pp. 31–33.

63. Ibid., pp. 33–34.

64. Ibid., p. 52. As early as 1913 Otto recognized that Nirvana was for Buddhists an object of value, indeed, "the value of all values." See Otto, "Parallelen und Wertunterschiede," p. 4.

65. Chapter 10 of *Das Heilige* is entitled "Das sanctum als numinoser Wert," in contrast to the English edition's "The Holy as a Category of Value." The English translation fails to make the distinction between these sufficiently clear in a number of places.

66. Otto, *Religious Essays*, pp. 38–39.

67. Ibid., pp. 25–26.

68. Ibid., p. 3.

69. Otto, *Sünde und Urschuld*, p. vii.

70. Otto, *Religious Essays*, p. 5.

71. Otto, *The Idea of the Holy*, p. 55. See also Rudolf Otto, *The Philosophy of Religion* (London: Williams and Norgate, 1931), p. 228; *India's Religion of Grace and Christianity Compared and Contrasted* (London: S.C.M. Press, 1930), pp. 13–14; *Mysticism East and West*, pp. 33–35.

72. Otto, "Parallelen und Wertunterschiede," p. 3.

73. Otto, *The Idea of the Holy*, p. 164.

74. The most readable and accessible of these various quests for the origin, and hence the essence, of religion remains Edward E. Evans-Pritchard, *Theories of Primitive Religion* (Oxford: Clarendon Press, 1965).

75. Otto, *The Idea of the Holy*, p. 110.

76. Ibid., p. 122.

77. Ibid.

78. Ibid., p. 132.

79. Ibid., p. 44.

80. Ibid., p. 123.

81. Ibid.

82. Ibid., p. 133.

83. See Walter Baetke, *Das Heilige im Germanischen* (Tübingen: J. C. B. Mohr, 1942), pp. 40–44.

84. See Heinrich Frick, "Zur Diskussion um 'Das Heilige' nach Rudolf Otto," *Theologische Literaturzeitung* 69 (1944): 1–10.

85. Gustav Mensching, review of Baetke, *Das Heilige*, in *Theologische Literaturzeitung* 68 (1943): 12.

86. Joseph Geyser, *Intellekt oder Gemüt* (Freiburg im Breisgau: Herder, 1921); selections reprinted in *Die Diskussion um das Heilige*, ed. Carsten Colpe (Darmstadt: Wissenschaftliche Buchgesellschaft, 1977), p. 312.

87. Baetke, *Das Heilige*, p. 21. See also a letter from Bultmann to Otto, April 6, 1918, HS797/757; Troeltsch, "Zur Religionsphilosophie," p. 65; John Oman, *The Natural and the Supernatural* (Cambridge: Cambridge University Press, 1931), p. 61; Herbert J. Paton, *The Modern Predicament* (London: Allen and Unwin, 1955), p. 137; Malcolm Diamond, *Contemporary Philosophy and Religious Thought* (New York: McGraw-Hill, 1974), pp. 94–97; John M. Moore, *Theories of Religious Experience* (New York: Round Table Press, 1938), p. 93.

88. Otto, *Das Gefühl des Überweltlichen*, p. 327. See also Otto's notes to the English translation of *Kantisch-Fries'schen Religionsphilosophie*, in Hans-Walter Schütte, *Religion und Christentum in der Theologie Rudolf Ottos* (Berlin: de Gruyter, 1969), p. 124.

89. Otto, "Mythus und Religion," p. 305.

90. Otto, *Religious Essays*, p. 23.

91. Otto, *The Idea of the Holy*, p. 104. See also p. 138n2.

92. Rudolf Otto, "In the Sphere of the Holy," *The Hibbert Journal* 31 (1932–33): 416.

93. Ibid., p. 413.

94. Letter from Edmund Husserl to Otto, March 5, 1919, HS797/794.

Chapter 4

1. Rudolf Otto, *The Idea of the Holy* (Oxford: Oxford University Press, 1958), p. 5.

2. See, e.g., Paul Seifert, *Die Religionsphilosophie bei Rudolf Otto* (Düsseldorf: G. H. Nolte Verlag, 1936), pp. 90–91.

3. Hans-Walter Schütte, *Religion und Christentum in der Theologie Rudolf Ottos* (Berlin: de Gruyter, 1969), p. 129.

4. Paul Tillich, "Die Kategorie des 'Heiligen' bei Rudolf Otto," *Theologische Blätter* 2 (1923): 11.

5. Theodor Siegfried, epilogue to Rudolf Otto, *Freiheit und Notwendigkeit, ein Gespräch mit Nicolai Hartmann über Autonomie und Theonomie der Werte* (Tübingen: J. C. B. Mohr, 1940), p. 33.

6. Rudolf Otto, *Sünde und Urschuld* (München: C. H. Beck, 1932), p. 190. See also Otto, *The Idea of the Holy*, p. 109.

7. Friedrich Heiler in *Münchner Neueste Nachrichten* 79 (1926) argues that with *Das Heilige* something "quite new" begins. And Ernst Troeltsch, "Zur Religionsphilosophie," *Kant-Studien* 23 (1919): 76, talks of a "total about-face."

8. Epilogue to F. D. E. Schleiermacher, *Über die Religion: Reden an die Gebildeten unter ihren Verächtern* (Göttingen: Vandenhoeck und Ruprecht, 1899), p. xxix.

9. Rudolf Otto, "Parallelen und Wertunterschiede im Christentum und Buddatum," OA351, p. 2.

10. Rudolf Otto, "Parallels in the Development of Religion East and West," *Transactions of the Asiatic Society of Japan* 40 (1912): 158.

11. Rudolf Otto, "Parallelen der Religionsentwicklung," *Frankfurter Zeitung*, March 31 and April 1, 1913, p. 4.

12. Friedrich Delekat, "Rudolf Otto und das Methodenproblem in der heutigen systematischen Theologie," *Die christliche Welt* 44 (1930): 4.

13. See, e.g., Sören Holm, "Apriori und Urphänomen bei Rudolf Otto," in *Rudolf Otto's Bedeutung für die Religionswissenschaft und die Theologie Heute*, ed. Ernst Benz (Leiden: Brill, 1971), pp. 70–83.

14. Ernst Troeltsch, "Der Selbstständigkeit der Religion," *Zeitschrift für Theologie und Kirche* 5 (1895): 361.

15. See especially Ernst Troeltsch, "Zur Frage des religiösen Apriori," in his *Gesammelte Schriften* (Tübingen: J. C. B. Mohr, 1913), II, 754–68.

16. Rudolf Otto, *The Philosophy of Religion* (London: Williams and Norgate, 1931), p. 18.

17. Ansgar Paus, *Religiöser Erkenntnisgrund: Herkunft und*

Wesen der Aprioritheorie Rudolf Ottos (Leiden: Brill, 1966), p. 135.

18. See John Clayton, "Can Theology be Both Cultural and Christian?" in *Science, Faith and Revelation*, ed. Bob E. Patterson (Nashville: Broadman Press, 1979), pp. 91–92.

19. Troeltsch, "Zur Religionsphilosophie," p. 70.

20. Otto, *The Idea of the Holy*, p. 109.

21. Ibid., p. 112.

22. Ibid.

23. Ibid., p. 36.

24. Ibid., p. 112.

25. Ibid., p. 113.

26. Ibid.

27. See especially Theodor Siegfried, "Theologie als Religionswissenschaft," *Zeitschrift für Theologie und Kirche* 19 (1938): 16–45; also his *Grundfragen der Theologie bei Rudolf Otto* (Gotha: Leopold Klotz Verlag, 1931).

28. Rudolf Otto, *Naturalism and Religion* (London: Williams and Norgate, 1907), p. 69.

29. Otto, *The Idea of the Holy*, p. 113.

30. Rudolf Otto, *Das Heilige: Über das Irrationale in der Idee des Göttlichen und sein Verhältnis zum Rationalen* (Breslau: Trewendt und Granier, 1917), p. 120.

31. Otto, *The Idea of the Holy*, p. 113.

32. Herbert J. Paton, *The Modern Predicament* (London: Allen and Unwin, 1955), p. 136. See also Friedrich K. Feigel, *"Das Heilige": Kritische Abhandlung über Rudolf Ottos gleichnamiges Buch* (Tübingen: J. C. B. Mohr, 1948), selections reprinted in *Die Diskussion um das Heilige*, ed. Carsten Colpe (Darmstadt: Wissenschaftliche Buchgesellschaft, 1977), p. 402.

33. Bernard Häring, "'Das Heilige' Rudolf Ottos in der neueren Kritik," *Geist und Leben* 24 (1951): 66. See also Joseph Geyser, *Intellekt oder Gemüt* (Freiburg im Breisgau: Herder, 1921), selections reprinted in *Die Diskussion um das Heilige*, ed. Carsten Colpe, pp. 319–20; Walter Baetke, *Das Heilige im Germanischen* (Tübingen: J. C. B. Mohr, 1942); Heinz E. Eisenhuth, *Der Begriff des Irrationalen als philosophisches Problem* (Göttingen: Vandenhoeck und Ruprecht, 1931), pp. 8–22; Seifert, *Die Religionsphilosophie*, pp. 77–83; Robert F. Davidson, *Rudolf Otto's Interpretation of Religion* (Princeton:

Princeton University Press, 1947), pp. 187–92; Malcolm Diamond, *Contemporary Philosophy and Religious Thought* (New York: McGraw-Hill, 1974), pp. 79, 407n14; Paton, *The Modern Predicament*, pp. 135–39; Joachim Wach, *Types of Religious Experience* (Chicago: University of Chicago Press, 1951), p. 222; John Oman, *The Natural and the Supernatural* (Cambridge: Cambridge University Press, 1931), p. 63; John P. Reeder, "The Relation of the Moral and the Numinous in Otto's Notion of the Holy," in *Religion and Morality*, ed. Gene Outka and John P. Reeder (Garden City: Doubleday-Anchor, 1973), pp. 255–92. This last-named essay is by far the best account available in English on schematization. I am indebted to it at a number of points.

34. Otto, *The Idea of the Holy*, p. 45.

35. Ibid. (my italics).

36. Rudolf Otto, *Das Heilige: Über das Irrationale in der Idee des Göttlichen und sein Verhältnis zum Rationalen* (München: C. H. Beck, 1963), p. 61. Otto, *Das Heilige* (1917, p. 49), reads, "nach Prinzipien inneren legitimer Verwandschaft und Zugehörigkeit." See also Otto, *The Idea of the Holy*, p. 45.

37. Otto, *The Idea of the Holy*, p. 45.

38. Ibid., p. 140.

39. Ibid., p. 141.

40. See, e.g., Paton, *The Modern Predicament*, pp. 138–39.

41. See, e.g., Otto, *The Philosophy of Religion*, pp. 56–57.

42. Otto, *The Idea of the Holy*, p. 109.

43. Ibid., p. 136.

44. Otto, *Das Heilige* (1917), p. 140. See also ibid., p. 137.

45. Otto, *Das Heilige* (1963), p. 165.

46. Ibid., p. 67.

47. See, e.g., the various articles on ethics cited in Chapter 1, n. 73. See also a number of unpublished lectures, two of which deal especially with ethics and religion—"Der Gotteswille" and "Sittengesetz und Gotteswille"—in the Rudolf Otto Archive. On these see Georg Wünsch, "Grundriss und Grundfragen der theologischen Ethik Rudolf Ottos," *Zeitschrift für Theologie und Kirche* 19 (1938): 46–70, and Karl Küssner, *Verantwortliche Lebensgestaltung* (Lüneberg: Metta-Kinau Verlag, n.d.).

48. Rudolf Otto, "Wert, Würde und Recht," *Zeitschrift für*

Theologie und Kirche 12 (1931): 58. See also Küssner, *Verant-wortliche Lebensgestaltung*, p. 17, and Wünsch, "Grundriss und Grundfragen," p. 51.

49. Küssner, *Verantwortliche Lebensgestaltung*, p. 18. See also Otto, "Wert, Würde und Recht," p. 58, and Wünsch, "Grundriss und Grundfragen," pp. 51–53.

50. Nicolai Hartmann, *Ethics* (New York: Macmillan, 1932), III, 260–74.

51. Rudolf Otto, *Freiheit und Notwendigkeit, ein Gespräch mit Nicolai Hartmann über Autonomie und Theonomie der Werte* (Tübingen: J. C. B. Mohr, 1940), p. 8.

52. Hartmann, *Ethics*, p. 265.

53. Otto, *Freiheit und Notwendigkeit*, p. 12. See also Küssner, *Verantwortliche Lebensgestaltung*, p. 170.

54. Otto, *Freiheit und Notwendigkeit*, p. 13.

55. Ibid., p. 15.

56. Ibid., p. 12. See also Otto, *The Idea of the Holy*, pp. 101, 90–91; cf. p. 107.

57. Otto, *Freiheit und Notwendigkeit*, p. 9. See also Otto, *The Idea of the Holy*, Ch. 8.

58. Otto, *Freiheit und Notwendigkeit*, pp. 10–11.

59. Ibid., p. 15. See also Küssner, *Verantwortliche Lebensges-taltung*, p. 31.

60. Otto, *Freiheit und Notwendigkeit*, p. 18.

61. Ibid., p. 15. See also Küssner, *Verantwortliche Lebensges-taltung*, p. 84, and Wünsch, "Grundriss und Grundfragen," pp. 58–59.

62. Cf. Reeder, "The Relation of the Moral and the Numinous," pp. 288–92. He fails here to distinguish between *das* Heilige and *der* Heilige and therefore attributes the source of moral value only to the nonrational element in the divine, not to the combined rational and nonrational Holy.

63. Küssner, *Verantwortliche Lebensgestaltung*, p. 84. See also p. 170.

64. Otto, *Freiheit und Notwendigkeit*, p. 17.

65. Ibid.

66. Ibid., p. 18. See also Küssner, *Verantwortliche Lebensgestaltung*, p. 33.

67. Otto, *Das Heilige* (1936), p. 67, e.g., suggests the nonra-tional side of the Holy as the source of moral value, whereas

Otto, *Freiheit und Notwendigkeit,* pp. 10–11, relates it to the combined Holy.

68. But see, e.g., Reeder, "The Relation of the Moral and the Numinous," pp. 291–92.

69. Otto, *The Idea of the Holy,* p. 143.

70. Ibid., p. 145.

71. Ibid., p. 168.

72. Ibid., p. 146. The experience to which Schleiermacher refers in the *Speeches on Religion* is an experience of the divine in phenomena; the experience described as "the feeling of absolute dependence" in *The Christian Faith* is, according to Otto, an inner one. See also Rudolf Otto, *Mysticism East and West* (New York: Macmillan, 1932), pp. 253–63.

73. Otto, *The Idea of the Holy,* p. 150.

74. Rudolf Otto, "Jakob Friedrich Fries' philosophischer Roman Julius and Evagoras," *Deutsche Literaturzeitung* 31 (1910): 2828; Otto, *The Idea of the Holy,* pp. 149–50.

75. See also Otto, *The Idea of the Holy,* p. 150.

76. Rudolf Otto, *Die historisch-kritische Auffassung vom Leben und Wirken Jesu* (Göttingen: Vandenhoeck und Ruprecht, 1901), p. 62.

77. Otto, *The Idea of the Holy,* p. 177.

78. Ibid. See also p. 122.

79. See Rudolf Otto, *Das Gefühl des Überweltlichen (Sensus Numinis)* (München: C. H. Beck, 1932), p. 79.

80. See, e.g., Karl Heim, "Ottos Kategorie des Heiligen und der Absolutheitsanspruch des Christusglaubens," *Zeitschrift für Theologie und Kirche* 1 (1920): 14–41.

81. Otto, *The Idea of the Holy,* p. 158.

82. Ibid., p. 156.

83. Ibid., pp. 169–70.

84. Ibid., p. 170.

Chapter 5

1. Rudolf Otto, *The Philosophy of Religion* (London: Williams and Norgate, 1931), p. 225.

2. Rudolf Otto, *Vischnu-Nārāyana: Texte zur indischen Gottesmystik* (Jena: E. Diederich, 1917), p. 7.

3. Rudolf Otto, *Aufsätze das Numinose betreffend* (Stuttgart/Gotha: Verlag Friedrich Andreas Perthes, 1923), p. 136. See also Rudolf Otto, *Religious Essays* (London: Oxford University Press, 1931), p. 30.

4. Rudolf Otto, "Parallels in the Development of Religion East and West," *Transactions of the Asiatic Society of Japan* 40 (1912): 154. See also Rudolf Otto, "Parallelen und Wertunterschiede im Christentum und Buddatum," OA351, p. 2.

5. Rudolf Otto, "Parallelen der Religionsentwicklung," *Frankfurter Zeitung*, March 31 and April 1, 1913, p. 1–16. See also the shorter and slightly altered English translation, "Parallels and Convergences in the History of Religions," in Otto, *Religious Essays*, pp. 95–109, and Otto, *Das Gefühl des Uberweltlichen*, pp. 282–305.

6. Otto, *Religious Essays*, p. 96.

7. Otto, "Parallelen," p. 16.

8. Ibid.

9. OA201.

10. Friedrich Heiler, "Vom Wesen der Religion," *Kölnische Zeitung*, April 24, 1937, OA527.

11. Emil Brunner, "Theologie und Philosophie," *Literarischer Anzeiger* 12 (1926), OA94.

12. Otto, *Aufsätze*, p. 72.

13. Ibid.

14. Rudolf Otto, *Das Heilige: Über das Irrationale in der Idee des Göttlichen und sein Verhältnis zum Rationalen* (Breslau: Trewendt und Granier, 1917), p. 89n1. See also Rudolf Otto, *The Idea of the Holy* (Oxford: Oxford University Press, 1958), pp. 85n1, 21–22, 194; Otto, *Aufsätze*, pp. 65, 119, 125. But cf. Rudolf Otto, *Das Heilige* (München: C. H. Beck, 1963), p. 106, where the same description is offered "not as an adequate definition but as an essential trait of mysticism."

15. Rudolf Otto, *Mysticism East and West* (New York: Macmillan, 1932), p. 41. See also p. 44 and Otto, *The Idea of the Holy*, p. 30.

16. Otto, *Mysticism East and West*, pp. 34–35.

17. Ibid., pp. 33–34.

18. Ibid., p. 67.

19. Ibid., p. 68.

20. See also ibid., p. 267.

21. Ibid., p. 69. See also pp. 267–68.

22. Ibid., pp. 70–71.

23. Ibid., p. 71.

24. Ibid., pp. 253–63, 268.

25. Ibid., p. 268.

26. Ibid., p. 100.

27. Ibid.

28. Ibid., p. 160.

29. Ibid., p. 275 (my italics).

30. Ibid., pp. 277–78.

31. Ibid., p. 278.

32. Otto, *The Idea of the Holy*, p. 194.

33. Otto, *Mysticism East and West*, p. 280.

34. Otto, *Das Heilige* (1963), pp. 138–39. The final sentence does not appear in the ninth edition from which the English translation was made.

35. Otto, *Mysticism East and West*, p. 187.

36. Ibid., p. 210.

37. Ibid., p. 214. See also Otto, *The Idea of the Holy*, pp. 204–7; Rudolf Otto, *Sünde und Urschuld* (München: C. H. Beck, 1932), pp. 178–84. On the originality of Otto's work on the connection of Luther to German mysticism, see Ernst Benz, "Rudolf Otto in seiner Bedeutung für die Erforschung der Kirchengeschichte," *Zeitschrift für Kirchengeschichte* 56 (1937): 383–95.

38. Otto, *Mysticism East and West*, p. 223.

39. Ibid., p. 225.

40. Ibid., p. 235.

41. For a delightful account of Otto's first encounter with Rāmānuja's thought during his first trip to India, see Otto, "Parallelen," pp. 1–4. It also appears in Otto, *Vischnu-Nārāyana*, pp. 1–4.

42. Hans Rollmann, "Rudolf Otto and India," *Religious Studies Review* 5 (1979): 199, contains an excellent summary of Otto's work on the Indian traditions and an exhaustive bibliography of Otto's published writings on India and Japanese Buddhism.

43. Rudolf Otto, "Rāmānuja," *Die Religion in Geschichte und Gegenwart*, 2nd ed. (Tübingen: J. C. B. Mohr, 1929–31), IV, 1692–94. Otto's *Die Gnadenreligion Indiens und das Christen-*

tum also received a number of favorable reviews, notably one from Helmuth von Glasenapp (OA99).

44. Rollmann, "Rudolf Otto," p. 200.

45. See, e.g., Rudolf Otto, *India's Religion of Grace and Christianity Compared and Contrasted* (London: S.C.M. Press, 1930), p. 17; Rudolf Otto, *Siddhānta des Rāmānuja: Ein Text zur indischen Gottesmystik* (Jena: E. Diederich, 1917), pp. 4–6.

46. Otto, *India's Religion of Grace*, p. 14.

47. Ibid., p. 21.

48. Ibid., p. 66.

49. Ibid.

50. Otto, *The Idea of the Holy*, p. 168.

51. See, e.g., Rudolf Otto, *The Kingdom of God and the Son of Man* (Grand Rapids, Mich.: Zondervan Press, 1938), p. 104. In his early work on Jesus, the Kingdom is merely an internal event and Christ's message is primarily ethically intended. See, e.g., Rudolf Otto, *The Life and Ministry of Jesus* (Chicago: Open Court, 1908), pp. 55–56, 59, 63, 71, 74. For a useful summary in English of Otto's *The Kingdom of God*, see Werner G. Kümmel, *The New Testament: The History of the Investigation of Its Problems* (London: S.C.M. Press, 1973), pp. 386–89. In spite of the insights into the nature of Jesus' preaching of the Kingdom of God, the book suffers from two main defects: first, a dubious synoptic theory which Otto derived from Wilhelm Bussmann; second, Otto's view that the key to the figure of Jesus is to be found above all in the Book of Enoch. *The Kingdom of God* had, as a consequence, a mixed reception. It was favorably reviewed by, for example, Heinrich Frick, Otto's successor at Marburg, in "Wider die Skepsis in der Leben-Jesu-Forschung: R. Ottos Jesus-Buch," *Zeitschrift für Theologie und Kirche* 16 (1935): 1–20, but it was harshly treated by Rudolf Bultmann in "Reich Gottes und Menschensohn," *Theologische Rundschau* 9 (1935): 1–35. This was in part, undoubtedly, because of the polemical stance taken by Otto against Bultmann's own position. On this, see Martin Dibelius's review in *Göttingische Gelehrte Anzeigen* 6 (1935): 210 (OA116); Otto, *The Kingdom of God*, pp. 51, 58.

52. Otto, *India's Religion of Grace*, p. 70.

53. See ibid., p. 75.

54. Otto, "Parallelen und Wertunterschiede," p. 32. See also ibid., p. 74.

55. Otto, *India's Religion of Grace*, p. 82.

56. Ibid., pp. 102–3. See also Otto, "Parallelen und Wertun-terschiede," p. 32; Otto, *The Idea of the Holy*, pp. 172–73.

57. This tendency can be traced to Ninian Smart, *Reasons and Faiths* (London: Routledge and Kegan Paul, 1958). Subse-quent usage of "numinous experience," especially among phi-losophers of religion, is always in a theistic context, and as such is contrasted with mystical experience.

58. On mysticism and *mysterium*, see Otto, *The Idea of the Holy*, p. 29. On *fascinans*, see p. 39; on *tremendum*, see pp. 17, 21, 24. See also *Aufsätze*, pp. 65–70, 119–32.

59. Otto, *Aufsätze*, pp. 71–107.

60. See also, Otto, *Mysticism East and West*, p. 216.

61. Otto, *Aufsätze*, p. 71. See also p. 77.

62. Otto, *The Idea of the Holy*, p. 203. See also pp. 198, 201.

63. Ibid., p. 202. See also p. 199 and Otto, *Siddhānta des Rāmānuja*, p. 2.

64. Otto, *The Idea of the Holy*, p. 1. See also p. 75.

65. Ibid., p. 173.

66. See Otto, *Das Gefühl des Überweltlichen*, pp. 3, 63.

67. Otto, *The Idea of the Holy*, pp. 141–42. See also pp. 56–82.

Bibliography of Otto's Works in English

Naturalism and Religion. London: Williams and Norgate, 1907.

The Life and Ministry of Jesus. Chicago: Open Court, 1908.

"Parallels in the Development of Religion East and West." *Transactions of the Asiatic Society of Japan* 40 (1912): 153–58.

The Idea of the Holy. Oxford: Oxford University Press, 1923.

Christianity and the Indian Religion of Grace. Madras: Christian Literature Society for India, 1928.

India's Religion of Grace and Christianity Compared and Contrasted. London: S.C.M. Press, 1930; New York: Macmillan, 1930.

The Philosophy of Religion. London: Williams and Norgate, 1931; New York: Richard R. Smith, 1931.

Religious Essays. London: Oxford University Press, 1931.

"Der Sensus Numinis as the Historical Basis of Religion." *The Hibbert Journal* 30 (1931–32): 283–97, 415–30.

Mysticism East and West. New York: Macmillan, 1932.

"In the Sphere of the Holy." *The Hibbert Journal* 31 (1932–33): 413–16.

The Kingdom of God and the Son of Man. Grand Rapids, Mich.: Zondervan Press, 1938.

The Original Gita: The Song of the Supreme Exalted One. London: Allen and Unwin, 1939.

"Introduction" to F. D. E. Schleiermacher, *On Religion: Speeches to Its Cultured Despisers.* New York: Harper & Row, 1958.

Index

DATE DUE